THE TEMPLE IN NOAH'S ARK

FROM CHAOS TO ORDER

DR. DINAH DYE

The Temple Revealed in Noah's Ark: From Chaos to Order

By Dinah Dye

Foundations in Torah Publishing

Unless otherwise noted, Scripture quotations are taken from the Tree of Life Version (TLV) Messianic Jewish Family Bible Society. Copyright © 2015.

ISBN 978-0-9972410-6-8

Visit the author's website at www.FoundationsInTorah.com

For those in the
Underground Church
who live under
oppression and
tyranny...

The people of the United States of America
are the last best hope for freedom on earth.
May they learn your stories and prepare
for what's ahead.

"These are the times that try men's souls. The summer
soldier and the sunshine patriot will, in this crisis,
shrink from the service of their country: but he that
stands it now, deserves the love and thanks of man
and woman. Tyranny, like hell is not easily conquered;
yet we have this consolation with us, that the harder
the conflict, the more glorious the triumph."

THOMAS PAINE, THE CRISIS

ACKNOWLEDGMENTS

Sarah Hawkes Valente: Chief among editors
David Farley: Mechanicals/Graphic design
Robin Hanley: Cover designer
Tyler Dawn Rosenquist: Content Editor
Hannah Romero: Proofreader
Margo Doll: Proofreader

CONTENTS

PROLOGUE

Your throne is established of old:
You are from everlasting
The floods have lifted up, O Lord
The floods have lifted up their voice,
The floods lift up their waves
The Lord on high is mightier
than the sound of many waters,
Yea, than the mighty waves of the sea.
(Psalm 93:2-5)

Elohim spread His celestial robe over the cosmos to fashion a heavenly tent. The master architect re-measured the heavens, re-calculated the firmament, and counted out additional galaxies. He stretched His measuring rod over the entire earth to verify its dimensions. He re-set the boundary lines of His sacred space. After re-installing bars and gates that separated the waters above from those below, *Elohim* once again declared His sovereignty over the cosmos. The world was now firmly re-established. His kingdom reigned over all. Surrounding His Throne of Glory, Heaven's hosts, in piercing tones, proclaimed, "Yours is the Kingdom and the Power and the Glory forever! From everlasting to everlasting, You are God!"

Adam and Eve, the first of *Elohim's* kings, had violated the terms of the royal covenant by eating fruit from the forbidden tree. In doing so, they contaminated *YHWH's* creation. For "to take the fruit" and "to eat the fruit" signaled a human king's craving to become divine—something the gods continually encouraged. In an attempt to deify himself by usurping *Elohim's* moral and ethical authority, Adam enacted his own justice. Chaos ensued. Adam and Eve lost their humanity and were sent into exile where they lived as slaves, forced to toil in the fields of the nations' gods and kings.

Elohim searched for a righteous king to task with rebuilding His earthly House, as the kings of the earth had thoroughly contaminated it with their lawbreaking and violence. Man's moral and ethical failure had utterly corrupted creation. *Elohim* determined to begin anew by bringing ruin upon all of Earth's inhabitants. Only one man and his family would be spared.

Elohim chose Noah—tenth in the line from Adam. He declared him *tamim*: complete. Noah had cut a royal covenant with God, and it was credited to him as righteousness. As *Elohim's* newly adopted Son of God, Noah inherited His Father's vocation of master carpenter. He was blessed with wisdom, knowledge, and divine skill in all the building trades. *Elohim* provided Noah with the blueprints necessary to rebuild the fallen tabernacle.

Noah's tri-level, boat-shaped sanctuary would be the architectural embodiment of a world mountain. Though built by human hands, it would be a place set apart and protected by God. Called the Heavens and the Earth, it would reside where Heaven and Earth joined as one. The mountain/sanctuary was designed to house the Divine Presence during times of great distress on Earth.

Wood was provided from the trunk of the Tree of the Knowledge of Good and Evil—sometimes referred to as the Tree of Justice. Its branches brimmed with swollen clusters of luscious fruit; its majestic boughs stretched longingly towards the heavens. The tree's generous foliage provided shade for the birds of the air who dwelled under *Elohim's* protective sovereignty. Its satiny, olive-colored leaves were said to impart godly wisdom to kings to assist them in governing the earth's inhabitants.

Noah overlaid the inside walls and floors with planks from the great cedars of the forest groves in Lebanon. He sealed the outside with pitch—bitumen from the seepage of the Euphrates River. He constructed a grand entryway modeled after the portal in the firmament. The entrance was carved from cypress trees which served as the gateway to Paradise. Noah carved two royal cherubim into the lintels of the ark's fifteen-cubit opening. Inside, a winding staircase connected all three levels. *Elohim* set apart the uppermost chamber as the family's personal quarters. There, Noah would perform the services of the High Priest: mediating on behalf of his family inside while atoning for those outside who had broken the covenant.

A wide array of paired animals filled the boat's middle level just as they had filled the earth during creation. As flashes of lightning streaked across a darkened sky and peals of thunder reverberated through heaven's corridors, the family of eight solemnly entered the boat-shaped sanctuary. Then *Elohim* sealed up the door of the ark so no one else could enter. Thus, on the first day of the first month, in Noah's sixth hundredth year, the sanctuary was finished.

Elohim swung open the firmament's hinged windows. At His command, the four winds of heaven were released as divine instruments to mete out judgment and reverse the created order. Thick, foreboding clouds garmented the earth like swaddling cloths. Then the fountains of the deep burst forth from the abyss. Rivers gushed from valley floors with razor-like force cutting channels into the mountains. Chaos was loosed from the deep. Rain pelted the earth for forty days and forty nights as the seas swelled and churned in an unrelenting assault.

A mighty wind pushed foam-tossed swells against the ark, threatening to break it apart. Violent waves battered the structure continuously for over a month, but chaos could not penetrate its boundary. As the ark's inhabitants were held safely inside, the flood waters rose to smother the earth and to snuff out the very memory of all covenant breakers.

Dwarfed by the endless sea, the immense-sized boat was lifted by the surge of the storm until it was fifteen cubits above the world's tallest peaks. As the boat ascended into the Presence of God, a heavenly chorus sang the fifteen Songs of Ascent. Above the raging of the storm, rich angelic tones could be heard inside the ark's upper chamber. Noah and his family slept peacefully in their inner sanctum immersed in the radiance of the Divine Presence. *Elohim* had personally installed a *zohar*, a window-like portal, that allowed light to penetrate their compartment and envelope the family in God's glory.

After a time, *Elohim* caused an east wind to pass over the face of the earth. He ordered the fountains of the deep to slowly return to the abyss. When the skies had cleared, a dove was sent forth from the boat sanctuary. She hovered over the receding waters and then encircled the earth seven times. She returned to her nest carrying a torn olive leaf which confirmed to Noah that the waters of chaos had indeed been pushed back. A seed had survived, sprouted, and taken root in the earth to become a mighty olive tree, foreshadowing the eternal dynasty of King David.

The ark came to rest on the mountains of Ararat—the headwaters for the Euphrates River. The name Ararat signified that the curse had been reversed. On the seventeenth day, a day commemorated as First Fruits to *Elohim*, Noah's family celebrated their deliverance from death. Victory was declared over the nations and over the deep. *Elohim* raised His invisible hand and removed the ark's impenetrable door so the royal family could exit. A sign appeared in the clouds; a rainbow-colored arc connected Heaven and Earth. The family rejoiced in *Elohim's* rulership over the cleansed planet.

Noah stood motionless in awe of his God who had preserved and protected his life. He bowed in humble gratitude before the One who had delivered his family from the wrath meted out to the world. It was on the seventh day that Noah, whose name means "rest," brought order to the world and took his seat on the throne atop Ararat. His work could now resume. His family would bear fruit, multiply, fill, and subdue the entire world. They would expand God's Kingdom through righteousness and justice. And so, with clean hands and a pure heart, Noah chiseled out stones for an altar he would build at the entrance to his tri-level sanctuary.

In the fields adjacent to his mountain home, Noah transplanted his father's choice grape vine and began to tend his vineyard. In time, the entire region would become the cradle for winemaking. Noah dug a foundation, cleared out the stones, and built a winepress along with a tower so his family could guard the ripening grape harvest. In his role as chief vintner, Noah meticulously cultivated the vines he had inherited from his father. He enjoyed the transition from sanctuary building to royal gardening. With *shalom* upon the earth and *Elohim's* king seated on the throne, the days of exile from the Presence of God were over—for now.

CHAPTER ONE

FOUNDATIONS

For Adonai Elyon is awesome,
A great King over all the earth.
He subdues peoples under us,
And nations under our feet.
God has gone up amidst shouting,
Adonai amidst the sound of the shofar.
For God is the King of all the earth.
God reigns over the nations.
God sits upon His holy throne.
Psalm 47.3-4,6,8a-9

The story of Noah's Ark is one of the Bible's best-known. For many, it evokes memories of Sunday school children plastering felt figures on flannel boards or coloring cartoon activity pages. Modern explorers tout aerial photos of Mount Ararat in Turkey's Agri province to prove the object they say is Noah's Ark. A Christian theme park in Kentucky features a life-sized replica of the ark as its main display, billing it as an engineering marvel that will amaze visitors.

Is Noah's Ark a quaint bedtime story? A major scientific marvel? An allegory? Was there a flood that covered the entire earth? Did a man named Noah build an extremely large boat and fill it with animals? Did the entire human race, save eight, drown in floodwaters?

Most scholars view the story of Noah metaphorically. Creationists attempt a more scientific approach. Prophecy buffs identify the flood with the end of the world, while churchgoers assume the story is literal even if it doesn't quite make sense. Clearly, the Biblical writers considered the flood and the preceding building of the ark to be highly significant events. After all, the story covers four full chapters in Genesis (6-9) while the creation account is told in only one! So, what were the ancient writers trying to communicate? How should modern readers approach the story?

The Temple Revealed in Noah's Ark: From Chaos to Order seeks to examine Noah, the ark, and the flood from an ancient Near Eastern cultural and historical perspective. It challenges the reader to think differently about the text and to go beyond the confines of our western, theological mindset. Themes such as creation and order, kingship, chaos, and tyranny will be discussed.

The book takes the reader on a journey through the early Genesis narratives (4-11) to discover that the cosmos is a kingdom, the mountain is the center of government, divine kingship brings order, the ark/sanctuary is the bulwark against chaos, and the vineyard is a new creation environment. Fictional vignettes about the lives of Cain, Lamech, and Noah are included to help the reader appreciate kingship in the ancient world. Ultimately, the book explores how *YHWH* dethrones the gods/rulers (past and future) and the chaos they create to restore order for humanity.

A Note About Myths

Our modern view of mythology can limit our understanding of the Biblical texts. For the ancients, myths were how they explained the world around them. Modern readers view myths as false representations of the truth, fictional accounts, or quaint stories that have nothing to do with reality—simply the stuff of legends and folklore within the life of primitive cultures. Richard Averback explains, "We are not talking here about a limited kind of 'primitive mentality' that treats the ancients as ignorant prescientific people. They did not lack the ability to think in empirical and sophisticated ways" (2004: 331).

Myths were stories written in symbolic form designed to convey deep truths about reality. They were dramatizations, not narratives, presenting historical and factual information. "Myths can be summarized as an attempt to understand and impart meaning to reality in narrative and symbolic form without regard to empiricist concerns" (Silverman 2013: 5).

Myths reveal the essence of ancient cultures: what their gods were like, who they were as humans, where they came from literally and culturally, and how they saw themselves in the big picture. Myths communicated, and still communicate, universal timeless truths that ancient cultures embraced in an effort to make sense of their world. Myths are simply windows into that reality.

Margaret Barker explains that myths were not passed down as primitive history but rather as statements about current realities presented in symbolic or narrative form. These symbols functioned as building blocks that fit together to reveal "real" life. "The myth is an expression of man's understanding of reality" (Childs 2009: 17). Though a myth can be a fictional story, it does not follow that the reality of that story is false. Nor does mythological type language reduce the Bible to fiction. The language of myth is designed to help us make sense of what the text is saying, as well as what the author is trying to accomplish.

With this understanding in mind, we can safely say that Genesis 1-11 is rich with mythological stories. Some scholars have suggested these chapters were written in reaction to myths the surrounding nations had embraced. The goal of the Genesis writers, they say, was to destruct as well as destroy popular mythical stories. For example, the biblical creation account may have been written to deconstruct *Enuma Elish*, Babylon's creation myth; Noah and the Flood may have been written to deconstruct the *Epic of Gilgamesh*, a popular ancient flood myth.

Creation and Noah's Flood as put forth by the Bible set up a radically different worldview than that presented by the nations' myths. The biblical accounts created an alternate reality by which God's people could orient themselves within their everyday experience. These accounts were not meant to convey a timeline as much as they were meant to tell people who they were, what their God was like, and how they could relate to Him and the world (Van Oudtshoorn 2015: 3,18).

The Genesis cosmology (the study of the origins of the universe) represented a break from the Ancient Near East (ANE) cosmologies. The biblical writers did not merely rewrite existing myths; they set them within a new framework to enable Israel to think differently about their own world. This world, Israel's world, was differentiated by an emphasis on historical events in which God miraculously intervened and overcame real obstacles as part of His promise to His people. Myths that were popular in the surrounding nations had to be challenged, reworked, and transformed in order to align with God's revelation of Himself to Israel.

The Genesis myths were set within an historical framework but were retold so Israel could think differently about her world and her place in history. This allowed Israel to understand she was no longer at the mercy of the tyrannical gods of the nations but was now a citizen of a kingdom under the merciful and just reign of *YHWH*. Israel needed to recognize that she was created by God to bless the other nations. "Most of the Bible is historically and contextually grounded, this is a good indication that we may be dealing with a form of truth seeking to inform and shape Israel's worldview in contrast to that of the other nations" (Van Oudtshoorn 2015: 7).

Scholars, such as John Van Seters, suggest Genesis (1-11) is "history writing" that is presented as "an integral part of Israel's history" calling it historical in terms of mythology (1992: 188-93). According to Richard Averbeck, this history writing presents *YHWH* as the One True God who stands outside of the world and outside history.

At the heart of complex ancient mythology was the temple. Early on, Christians attached great importance to the Temple with its unique rituals and ceremonies, finding creation embedded in the symbolism (Barker 2010: 18). Barker also reminds us that "[t]he Temple is like an ancient tapestry; in some parts the picture has faded, in others the threads are no longer clear... it is impossible to understand the temple using twentieth century post-enlightenment ways"(2008: 57,58).

Central to the biblical creation story was the necessity of restoring God's Presence to His people—the purpose of Israel's temple rebuilding program. The design of *YHWH's* House was based on the original pattern of Eden's garden which was itself patterned after the cosmos. Noah's Ark, the Tents of the Patriarchs, the Tabernacle in the wilderness, Solomon's Temple, Ezekiel's Temple, the Second Temple, and Revelation's Temple were all later representations of the original blueprint of the garden sanctuary.

The Cosmic Kingdom

The ancients viewed the cosmos as a kingdom ruled by a king. Their perspective was not scientific, nor was it historical. It wasn't even religious. It was governmental. In the Bible, the expression "Kingdom of Heaven" (not found in the Hebrew Scriptures) was synonymous with the rule of God on Earth. The Kingdom was not located in an alternate universe or some remote corner of Heaven. It was God, as master craftsman, who built the cosmic temple by the word of His mouth. It was God as king, seated on His throne, who ruled over His creation. It was God as judge, and administrator, who brought order to the world and who exercised divine justice—conquering chaos to provide blessing, stability, and prosperity for His subjects.

"Creation itself is understood as a kind of Temple, a heaven-and-earth duality, where humans function as the 'image-bearers' in the cosmic Temple, part of the earth yet reflecting the life and love of heaven. This is how creation was designed to function and flourish: under the stewardship of the image-bearers" (Wright 2016: 76-77). Also, according to Wright, humans are called "[to] celebrate, worship, procreate, and take responsibility within the rich, vivid developing life of creation"(76-77). Creation was *YHWH's* Holy House where His image-bearers could approach Him in worship, for worship was the "telos" or the goal of His creation.

According to Dr. John Walton, the ancient writers showed how the world operated as a kingdom, not as a machine, and that certain details were not secretly hidden inside the text for later generations to discover. Walton writes, "Things worked the way they did because God made it that way and because He maintained the system" (Longman & Walton 2018: 8). Walton suggests it was not the literal, historical events about which men were inspired to write but rather the interpretation of those events (23). The Bible focuses, then, on what the writers understood or believed about those events.

Modern readers examine Scripture as though it were a scientific report filled with facts and figures. Peter Enns explains, "The Old Testament is not a treatise on Israel's history for the sake of history, and certainly not a book of scientific interest, but a document of self-definition and persuasion: Do not forget where we've been. Do not forget who we are—the people of God" (2012: 10). Noted astrophysicist Dr. Jennifer Wiseman captures the same sentiment: "You have to look at biblical literature from the perspective of when it was written, the original audience, the original languages, the original purposes... the message that was meant to be conveyed by it. The Bible's not a scientific text" (quoted in Horowitz 2018: 4).

ANE (Ancient Near East) literary works were highly visual. They were filled with figurative, imaginative, and metaphorical language. Like their ANE counterparts, the biblical writers utilized a variety of literary tools and devices to communicate. For example, the use of hyperbole may account for the flood story's perplexing details: the exaggerated life spans (Gen. 5), the extremely large boat for its time (Gen. 6.15), the catastrophic flood covering the entire earth (Gen. 7.17-21), and the annihilation of all mankind (Gen. 7.22-24). The flood story is rooted in an actual event, but that event is described using figurative language. The writer was not concerned with detailing specifics as much as pointing to the significance and meaning behind the event.

The purpose of employing hyperbole is to make a point. The dimensions of the ark were breathtakingly large for the day with nothing close to that size in the ancient world. It is possible the size and design were more rhetorical in nature—purposely meant to mirror a cosmic temple rather than an actual boat, since the average skin and reed boat that sailed in the marshes or along riverbanks at the time was barely ten feet long (Longman & Walton 2018: 38,39).

Yeshua (Hebrew name for Jesus) often employed hyperbole to reinforce his point. His messages were not intended as a list of rules or statements about theology. Most would agree that "hating" one's family was not meant to be taken literally. "If anyone comes to Me, and does not hate his own father, mother, wife, children, brothers and sisters—and yes, even his own life—he cannot be my disciple" (Luke 14.26). What was his point? It was that *Yeshua* should come before everything else! The same can be said for gouging out one's right eye or cutting off one's right hand and throwing it away as the appropriate response to lust (Matt. 5.29-30). Clearly, this is very graphic imagery used to make a point.

Faulconer suggests that applying a modern literal interpretation may result in, "robbing that event of its status as a way of understanding the world." The ancients believed "[the] scriptures were telling us the truth of the world, of its things, its events and its people—a truth that cannot be told apart from its situation in a divine, symbolic ordering" (2007: 426).

Peter Enns, in his article *When was Genesis Written and Why Does it Matter*, suggests the stories in Genesis weren't written to be mined for scientific facts. He claims that the accounts were written to explain the crisis Israel would later face: the Babylonian exile. Israel's exile resulted in the loss of their monarchy, their temple, their land, and ultimately their identity—the greatest shame possible in the ancient world. This was the seminal event in Israel's history and is an important lens through which to view Noah, the ark, and the flood. (The same can also be said about the Exodus from Egypt; both of these events can serve as filters for the flood story).

So how might Israel have reinterpreted the Genesis story for their situation in exile during the Babylonian captivity? Did the post exilic writers view the story of Noah through the lens of the Babylonian exile? How would they show that *YHWH* was still present in their situation—that the wonder-working God was still in their midst?

The Exilic Lens

Though Israel retold its story long before the Babylonian exile, the final formulation of the *Tanakh* (Hebrew Scriptures) didn't take place until the post-exilic period (538 BCE to 1 CE). The exile was likely a key factor in how the biblical writers interpreted Israel's earliest stories, especially those told in Genesis 1-11. Recent scholarship suggests the writers codified the final version in response to the exile. Peter Enns concludes, "Israel's moment of national crisis drove theologians to engage their past history creatively. The trauma of the exile was the driving factor in the creation of what has come to be known as 'the Bible'"(2012: 11). Shaye J.D. Cohen explains it was Second Temple Judaism that created the Bible and devoted enormous energies to its interpretation. This process was called canonization (2014: 11). The Babylonian exile was arguably *the* most traumatic and influential event in Israel's history. Modern Christianity has failed to recognize the exile's impact on the national psyche, the formulation of the Bible, and the overall message of Scripture.

Israel was sent into exile—taken captive by the Babylonians as a judgment for forgetting the Lord their God, His commandments, and the deeds He had done on their behalf. Israel's exile was the consequence of breaking covenant with *YHWH*, and it resulted in the upending of their governmental structure as well as their entire social order. Exile also meant a severing of Israel's ties with *YHWH*. Israel became a people without a land, a temple, or a king. Once the beneficiaries of a prosperous and flourishing nation that other nations envied, the Israelites were now reduced to a life of servitude in those nations. A conquered, dejected people—faceless, insignificant, displaced, and at the bottom of the Babylonian societal heap—they lost their history, their language, and their culture. As they served the Babylonian elites, they were constantly reminded that it was their oppressors who were now the image-bearers of the gods.

Israel's story tells of the struggle to become an independent nation with *YHWH* as their king. The monarchy, established once they conquered the land of Canaan and built a temple in Jerusalem, was to be an everlasting kingdom. The Hebrew Scriptures speak of Israel's patriarchal ancestors, of the Exodus, and of the establishment of the Torah. All these things led to Israel becoming a nation finally ruled by a faithful king enthroned in Jerusalem's Temple and overseeing a powerful military. Peter Enns explains that the nation in the land with a king and Temple is how the Israelites knew God was with them. The destruction of the Temple, the loss of the monarchy, the abandonment by the Divine Presence, and the surrendering to other nations as punishment was all together so unsettling it is metaphorically depicted in Scripture as "death." Exile is the most devastating thing that could have happened to the Chosen People.

Covenants were made between two parties in order to join their identities. *YHWH's* covenant promises to Israel meant Israel received the land as an inheritance along with a promise that a descendant would forever sit on the throne (2 Sam. 7.16). This covenant was confirmed through the exchange of names (such as the God of Israel and the Children of *YHWH*). Identity was one of the highest values in the ancient world; it defined a nation's very existence. A loss of identity meant humiliation and, with it, immeasurable shame in an honor/shame culture.

Because Israel's covenant with God granted them an identity that was honorable, the consequence of covenant-breaking was the loss of that identity. (In Scripture, a broken covenant is often tied to upheaval in the cosmic order that manifests as signs in the heavens: stars falling, constellations not giving light, the sun being darkened, or the moon turning to blood.) Israel would need to reconcile the reality of this loss with the possibility of still being called image-bearers of God. Could the idea of making a "man in our image and likeness" mean something new and different in the context of the Babylonian exile? Could it suggest that it was not the elite, the rich, or politically powerful in Babylon who were the image of God but rather, "ordinary human beings, men and women in partnership, who image God in the creation" (Walsh 2014: 21)?

Brian Walsh, suggests in his book *Subversive Christianity*, "[the] biblical perspective of human beings as God's stewardly image-bearers is best understood when read in the context of the Babylonian exile and Babylonian mythology" (27). The creation story as well as the Noah/flood story were likely written down during the exilic period and, according to Walsh, "functioned subversively" in that context. He notes that this idea isn't intended to dismiss the antiquity of the creation and the flood story in Genesis. It is a certainty that the Hebrew people had their own creation and flood stories long before the Babylonian exile.

Forming a collection of sacred books was a vehicle for restoring Israel's identity and renewing their covenant relationship with *YHWH*. Embellishing the past and reworking their stories allowed Israel to glory in *YHWH's* past deliverances and in the future redemption of their nation. "The Torah was likely completed in response to the exile, and the subsequent formation of the prophetic corpus and the 'writings' i.e. poetic and wisdom texts as bodies of religious literature is to be understood as a product of Second Temple Judaism [post-exilic period]. This suggests that by their intention, these materials are... an unintentional and coherent response to a particular circumstance of crisis... whatever older materials may have been utilized [and the use of old materials can hardly be doubted]" (Brueggemann: 1997: 74-75).

The exile was *the* turning point in Israel's religious history and where Judaism began. The final formation of the Bible helped recapture Israel's lost identity. It answered burning questions: Who are we? Who is our God? Are we still the people of a faithful God connected to the Israel of old? N.T. Wright explains that telling the story from a post-exilic perspective could help answer these questions, especially the question of whether we are still the people of God today? "Jewish eschatology in the Second Temple period focused on the hope that that which happened in the Babylonian exile, the triumph of paganism over Israel because of its sins, was still the dominant state of affairs but would at last be undone" (*Exile: A Conversation with N.T. Wright* 2017: 36). (The same can be said regarding Israel's response towards the Roman Empire in the book of Revelation.)

Genesis 1-11 was written to the despairing exiles to give them hope. "It cuts through the experience of exile to ground life in something more fundamental than the Babylonian experience—the creation itself" (Walsh 2014: 19). According to Walsh, creation was likened to a subversive act. In the face of a brutal empire such as Babylon, it was the One True God, the only king *YHWH*, who was THE God of the vanquished Israelites. The biblical creation story claimed it was He who was the final power and authority in Heaven, not the false god Marduk from the Babylonian creation myth. It is perhaps the case that both the creation story and the flood story were passed down to deconstruct the Babylonian myths in order to liberate a people in both physical and psychological captivity and to help give them an alternate world view (20). "The Babylonian creation myth with Marduk is not the story of the creation of the world; it is the story of the creation of the Babylonian state, told as if the state were the world" (Coote & Ord 2018: 46).

The church's view of Israel's history was also reshaped, but not so much from the crisis of the Babylonian exile. Instead, the New Testament writers revisited the Exodus story in which Israel was delivered from the slavery of Egypt's pagan world. Wright explains that they transformed Israel's story to emphasize what God was doing in *Yeshua* and how God himself has become king. The New Testament writers desired to answer the same question that the post-exilic Israelites had asked: what does it mean to be the people of God?

Creation was *the* message of liberation for Israel whether she was exiled in Babylon or Egypt or under Roman rule. In the Kingdom of God, Israel's value and worth was undeniable. The God of the universe would save and deliver His people so they could be transformed into His image. They would no longer be slaves—no longer at the mercy of the gods of their exilic existence.

Instead of drawing from the Babylonian exile, the New Testament writers drew from the Exodus perspective in which *Yeshua* became the focal point. Israel's creation story could also have been read as a condemnation of Egyptian mythology. The deliverance from Pharaoh and Egypt's gods as told in the Passover story was now revealed in the death and resurrection of *Yeshua* the Messiah. The Gospel accounts seemed to transform Israel's Exodus story to what God had done in and through *Yeshua*.

There are many instances in the Gospels that showcase the Exodus story. One example has *Yeshua* crossing the Sea of Galilee after a storm. He is headed to the region of the Gadarenes where he is met by two violent, demon-plagued men coming from the graveyard. "Now a large herd of pigs was feeding some distance away from them. The demons kept begging Him, 'If you drive us out, send us into the herd of pigs'... they went into the pigs and the whole herd rushed down the cliff into the sea and drowned" (Matt. 8.28-33).

Crossing the sea was imagery commonly used in the ANE for entering the abode of the underworld. This event in Matthew replays Pharaoh and his chariot army drowning in the sea. In ancient Egypt, the demon goddess Ammut, whose name means bone eater, was depicted as a pig who personified Nut the sky god. She was the demoness of death and the underworld who devoured souls as an act of divine retribution.

She is pictured with the head of a crocodile, the forequarters of a lion, the body of a leopard, and the hindquarters of a hippopotamus—all man-eaters. Ammut was often depicted crouching beside a lake of fire in the underworld. Anyone trying to win their way through the underworld needed to know the correct formula to ban pigs.

Yeshua delivered the two men from enslavement of the surrounding pagan cultures where they lived (the Decapolis region). He set these captives free from certain death by the "manslayer." Just as the herd of pigs rushed down the cliff into the sea and drowned, Pharaoh and his army drowned in the sea. "The Egyptians were fleeing from it, but *Adonai* overthrew them in the midst of the sea. The waters returned and covered the chariots, the horsemen, and the entire army of Pharaoh that went after them into the sea" (Ex. 14.27-28). For the two demon-possessed men, *Yeshua* was demonstrating that through him the pagan gods of the world's nations (Rome) had been upended and they were now free. Once again, creational order was restored from the chaos of the world's power.

The Wisdom To Build

In his book, *How the Bible Actually Works*, Peter Enns explains that the Bible's true purpose is to capture wisdom. He suggests the way we know God in our day and time is by gaining wisdom, and that it is God's wisdom that is necessary to mold us into His image. Enns further explains that the Bible is not meant to be an owner's manual or a rulebook but is instead the source of all wisdom. He writes, "Discerning how a commandment is to be obeyed…is an act of wisdom" (2019: 54). God's wisdom, when poured into the lives of His disciples, makes for mature, fruitful, and healthy citizens of the Kingdom. "To know God is to live with wisdom, who is more beautiful than the sun, and excels every constellation of the stars" (*Wisdom of Solomon* 7.29).

"The life of faith is the pursuit of wisdom" (Enns 2019: 46) which ultimately leads to knowledge and understanding of self. "God's presence comes not when we find the right passage, but when we embrace with courage—and anticipation—the way of wisdom"(47). The purpose of our lives, then, is to seek wisdom instead of indulging in mechanical obedience. Making the best choices for our lives always requires wisdom. Dr. John Walton describes wisdom as the pursuit of order as well as the pursuit of God who is the source and center of both.

Creation was an architectural concept synonymous with temple building that required a wise and knowledgeable artisan. "From eternity I [Wisdom] was appointed from the beginning, before the world began... when He laid out the earth's foundations—then I was the craftsman beside Him" (Prov. 8.23,30). "The divine building of the cosmic house by wisdom is the model for human house building" (Van Leeuwen 2007: 413). "By wisdom a house is built, by skill it is established. By knowledge (its) rooms are filled, with all [sorts of] wealth, precious and lovely" (Prov. 24.3-4).

In the creation account (Gen. 1.1-2.3), God is depicted as the master architect and builder who "constructs a three-story house—heaven, earth, seas—in six days, and then, upon completion, takes up residence enjoying Sabbath rest" (Morales 2017: 7). The cosmos is a tent with heavenly orbs embroidered on its fabric and a center pole called an *axis mundi*. This central axis connects Heaven and Earth, celestial bodies revolve around it, and the skies are stretched like a curtain inside the tent. According to Terrence Fretheim, creation was a building project resulting in heaven, earth, mountains, water, etc. as the world's infrastructure. It was the building of a cosmic triple-decker house, a temple God constructed with pillars, windows and doors. "[He] made the earth by his strength, established the world by His wisdom and by His skill stretched the heavens" (Jer. 10.12, 51.15).

The Psalmist described Creation in architectural terms, stating that the Lord set the earth on its pillars as a foundation (Ps. 104.5). Pillars were sunk into the earth, beams were laid over the waters, curtains were hung, and a cornerstone was set. The Hebrew word *banah*, "to build," is used as a noun and applied to various building trades: architect, smith, craftsman, artisan, carpenter. God measured, calculated, weighed, shaped, established, and set boundaries (Prov. 8.25-29). Who is like Him? "[W]ho has measured the waters in the palm of His hand, or measured out heaven with a span, or calculated the dust of the earth in a measure, or weighed the mountains in scales or the hills in a balance" (Is. 40.12)? The term "measured one," was later applied to Israel's kings—measured being synonymous with building and establishing a dynasty through royal seed. *YHWH* is the "workman who builds his house, inspects, pronounces upon his work and then takes his sabbath rest, the house itself, in as much as it is the house of God, being a temple" (Morales 2015: 41). "By employing building terminology in the Creation story, the priestly author has done nothing new, but has joined other biblical writers who describe the world as a building, the Creation as an act of building, and the Creator as a wise, knowledgeable and discerning architect" (Hurowitz 1992: 242).

Wisdom writings were not unique to Israel. ANE kings exercised wisdom by building and filling their temples. In ancient Mesopotamia, "building was a matter of divine command and agency and of human imitation of the divine wisdom in building" (Van Leeuwen 2007: 406). Israel's kings exercised God's wisdom through building and maintaining order in the Kingdom. House or temple building was a common expression that originated in ancient Mesopotamia (found in royal inscriptions common in the Neo-Assyrian period).

God imparted to King Solomon wisdom "as vast as the seashore" which "surpassed the wisdom of all the sons of the east and all the wisdom of Egypt" (I Kings 5.9-10). A wise king is "one who both creates order and brings his life into harmony with the established order of the universe" (Crenshaw 1976: 23). It was wisdom that created and sustained life in the empire.

In the ANE, wisdom produced order—order being the highest value in the ancient world. Human (the king's) wisdom was related to ordering and filling a temple. "Craftsmanship or skill in any area of human endeavor lies at the heart of biblical wisdom, because wisdom is a concept as wide and all-encompassing as creation, which in ancient thought included culture" (Van Leeuwen 2007: 419). Thus, ordering was tied to wisdom and connected to naming, counting, and bestowing identity. These elements brought into existence an ordered world from a non-existent or a non-ordered state which was the natural state of the world. A lack of godly wisdom resulted in confusion and brought the world into chaos.

Maintaining cosmic order was also tied to the architectural verb *khen*, meaning "to establish," from which comes *kohen* or priest. Priests were responsible for maintaining order and stability in God's sacred space which they did through acts of worship, ritual service, and ceremony. In the Temple, priests drew near to God as representatives of humanity so all could join with creation in worshipping *YHWH*.

In Noah's day, the world erupted in violence as a result of the evil inclinations of men's hearts. The earth's kings, called the wise ones, were morally depraved. They were deluded by their own wicked motivations. As God's wisdom was replaced by men's wisdom, violence and corruption became the order of the day. In order to reset the cosmos, the wisdom of God would need to be poured into His image-bearers who were called as a kingdom of priests to work in tandem with *YHWH* to restore order.

Noah, the son of the master craftsman, along with his sons, exercised this wisdom from God in their building of an ark, or a new creation temple for God's Presence. The ark was modeled after the cosmos. It was a three-leveled cosmic mountain structure that resembled heaven, earth, and sea. *Yeshua*, also the son of a carpenter, was filled with wisdom and knowledge to rebuild a new creation temple for God's presence in his body.

The Cosmic Mountain

The cosmic mountain was a powerful architectural symbol in the ANE world. Deemed the first place from which the material world was birthed, this mountain was said to hold the heavens, earth, and sea (underworld) together. Where Heaven and Earth met was imagined as a 'world mountain.' John Lundquist explains it this way: "the cosmic mountain as representing the primordial hillock which first emerged from the waters that covered the earth during the creative process" (1984: 57).

The holiest place in Egyptian Temples was the first mound of earth to have surfaced out of primordial waters (Wright 1944: 78). After witnessing new life as the Nile's annual floodwaters receded, the Egyptians connected the primordial mound to re-birth and re-creation of the world. This eventually gave way to the concept of the cosmic mountain representing the navel of creation, having been drawn out of water as the waters abated.

In ancient Mesopotamian building texts, Ugaritic mythology, and Egyptian temple texts, temples were identified with the cosmic mountain emerging from the waters of chaos. In the Babylonian creation myth, *Enuma Elish*, (dating from the reign 1119–1098 BCE of Nebuchadnezzar I) the waters of chaos subsided following the defeat of Tiamat by the god Marduk, and a dry mound appeared that transformed into a mountain.

Lundquist posits that the temple is the "architectural embodiment of the cosmic mountain" (1984: 59). During the creative process, the mound was separated out from the seas to become the first fixed place on Earth. Common to ANE cosmogony (that which concerns the origin of either the cosmos or the universe) was the separation of Heaven and Earth in the creation process. This separation also became a fundamental feature of Israelite cosmology: day from night, light from darkness, waters above from those below, seas from dry land, and woman from man all during the creation week.

The primordial mound or hillock transitioned from a natural mountain to a physical temple with well-defined boundaries and dedicated spaces. ANE cultures saw temples as the architectural expression of the primordial mound and the world mountain. Temples, in an effort to retain the mountain's natural character, were constructed of raw materials such as stone often quarried from the mountain itself. An example can be found in the book of Daniel (2:45) where a stone was cut from the mountain "not by hands" in order to crush the world's empires which were represented by iron, bronze, clay, silver, and gold—all mined by human hands. The cosmic mountain characterized the power base for ancient empires; temples, constructed on top of the mountain, housed the king's throne.

The top of the mountain featured the oracle of the god: a meeting place for deities and where divine decrees were issued (Clifford 1972: 3). Considered the divine abode of the gods, the mountaintop separated their work from the common everyday activities of the people. Visual manifestations of the deity appeared to those who ascended the mountain, especially the king upon his enthronement. At the summit, likened to heaven, the newly crowned king returned to the first fixed point of creation. "The architecture of the temple projects the building both as a mountain and as a structure based upon a heavenly model... the mountain and the temple are inseparable. The sacredness of the one [mountain] passes over onto and defines the sacredness of the other [temple]. All of those features which cause or create or determine sacredness of the mountain are attached to the temple and determine its architecture, its symbolism and its ritual" (Friedland and Hecht 1998: 140).

To the ancients, the cosmic mountain, the first fixed point in creation, was likened to a vertical pole with its base deep within the earth and its peak stretching towards the heavens. "The universe was thought of as a gigantic world-mountain stretching from the entrance of the subterranean abyss to the highest point of heaven and embracing all the inhabited world... the local sacred mountain was, therefore, a symbol, or representation of the cosmos which formed the true abode of the deity whom men worshipped" (Clements 1965: 2-3). The mountain became the focal point as the origin of the world (Morales 2012: 19). "Every ANE temple recalls a mountain but the first temple complex [garden of Eden] possessed a mountain in actuality" (Parry 1994: 133). The biblical Garden in Eden alluded to the presence of a mountain.

Ezekiel (28.11-18) speaks of a lament for the King of Tyre who was in Eden, the garden of God, and who was placed on the holy mountain of God. He was thrown out from the mountain for being a profane thing. "I threw you down to earth. Before kings I set you up as a spectacle." This is the ANE view of a divine king, seated on the throne of his temple/mountain sanctuary, being thrown down to Earth from Heaven as his empire and kingship was upended. In this case, the King of Tyre was removed from power in the face of the world's ruling kings only to return to mere mortal status on Earth.

Similarly, King Nebuchadnezzar is removed from power when *Adonai* comes against him. "*Adonai* has broken the rod of the wicked, the scepter of rulers... which ruled the nations in fury, with relentless persecution" (Is. 14.5,6b). Regarding His judgment against the King of Babylon, *Adonai* says, "How you have fallen from heaven, O Brightstar, son of the dawn! How you are cut down to the earth, you who made the nations prostrate!" (12-13). As with the King of Tyre, Nebuchadnezzar lost his kingdom and his divine status, having been brought down to She'ol: the lowest parts of the Pit.

The cosmic mountain was referred to as the *axis mundi* or the world's center. "The mountain represented order and definition, form and shape, amidst the waters of chaos" (Parry 1994: 137). The mountain symbolized "order, harmony, and beneficence" and was surrounded by "sacred trees with magical power" along with "four streams marking off the ancient quadrants of the created world" (Fishbane 1998: 111). Cosmic mountains, situated above the primordial waters, were the source of the sacred rivers that watered the four quarters of the earth. The rivers of Eden flowed downward suggesting Eden was located at an elevation higher than the surrounding territories. In Genesis (2.10-11), four rivers flowed out from Eden (the mountain) to water the garden. Considered the waters of life, the rivers gushed forth from inside the mountain or from its top and were thought to represent the upper waters of the firmament.

At the entrance to the Tent of Meeting, Moses spoke to the rock and water came forth for the community to drink (Num. 20.8). In Ezekiel's Temple, water flowed out from underneath the threshold of the House eastward (47.1) and eventually turned into a river with many trees on both banks. Every kind of tree grew and bore new fruit each month... "because its water flow[ed] out from the Sanctuary" (12). Cosmic mountains were later associated with the Tree of Life (Ps. 1) and with the throne of the king. Ultimately, Eden's mountain (which according to rabbinic tradition was later ascribed as the Temple Mount) became the refuge from the floodwaters.

The holiest place in Jerusalem's Temple was the site of the Foundation Stone, upon which the Ark of the Covenant sat inside the Holy of Holies. According to the *Zohar* (Jewish mystical commentary on the Torah called the Kabbalah),

"When the Holy One, blessed be He, was about to create the world, He detached one precious stone from underneath His throne of glory and plunged it into the abyss; one end of it remained fastened while the other end stood above...out of which the world started, spreading itself to the right and left and into all directions." Beneath this stone, which was called *Shetiyah* or stone of drinking, was hidden the source of all the springs and fountains from which the world drinks. The Talmud further explains that beneath this stone lies the abyss and the primeval waters of creation.

The mountain/temple was a refuge from the powers of chaos: the primeval waters. It served as the capstone that kept the waters of chaos at bay, making it possible for creation to take place. The mountain/temple prevented the threatening waters from surging forth from the abyss to which they had been imprisoned, thus preventing the work of creation from being thwarted or undone. In the ANE, raging waters were a symbol of the oppositional forces of life and a symbol of death when left uncontrolled. Morales notes that just as in other chaos sequences in the Hebrew Bible, the powers of destruction are conceived of as turbulent waters. The mountain represented a place of refuge from the waters of chaos that surrounded it—a place of protection from chaos and yet also the source for the world's rivers and springs.

For Israel, it was the Mountain of God that presented the ultimate bulwark against a mighty adversary. God's name, *El Shaddai*, was held to mean "the One of the mountain" or "God of the mountain" or even "Mountain-Dweller" (Bailey 1968: 434-438). "It will come to pass in the last days that the mountain of *Adonai's* House will stand firm as head of the mountains and will be exalted above the hills... Come let us go up to the mountain of *Adonai*, to the House of the God of Jacob" (Is. 2.2,3b)!

The concept of mountains symbolizing victory over the chaotic waters becomes important for understanding the story of Noah and the flood. As the turbulent waters receded and the mountains emerged, the ark came to rest atop Ararat. Rest signified that the king, Noah (whose name means rest), had ascended the mountain to the ark/sanctuary to take his seat on the throne. As the waters began to recede, the rebirth of the primordial mountain signified a new creation with both mountain and ark tied to the future renewal and rebuilding of the temple and the restoration of the monarchy.

Clearly, the cosmic mountain is much more than just a literary image. It was foundational for the development of the cult of Israel. The Mountain of God showed Israel that His sovereign kingdom maintained control over the seas—the primeval waters—represented by the nations of the world.

"Then I saw a new heaven and new earth; for the first heaven and the first earth had passed away and the sea was no more. Then he carried me away in the *Ruach* (spirit) to a great and high mountain, and he showed me the holy city, Jerusalem, coming down out of heaven from God, having the glory of God—her radiance like a most precious stone, like a jasper, sparkling like crystal" (Rev. 21.1,10-11).

Waters of Chaos

Most cultures have a flood story that reflects their common heritage. Stephanie Dalley (*Myths from Mesopotamia*) explains all flood stories derive from one Mesopotamian original that was told by travelers as they journeyed along the ancient caravan routes. The people knew floods were a destructive power capable of wiping out entire towns and cities, even civilizations. With so many towns located on the banks of the Tigris and Euphrates, flooding was a very real and constant threat. A number of scholars believe the Genesis flood story was inspired by a particularly memorable flooding event of the Tigris and Euphrates rivers (c. 2800 BCE) in which virtually all the cities were wiped out.

Noah's story is a historical event that uses figurative language to emphasize its "theological" significance rather than a story that outlines informational details. Walton suggests that the use of hyperbole permeates the flood account especially regarding the dimensions of the ark. Walton also posits that a boat the size and shape of the one outlined in Genesis would not be seaworthy (Longman & Walton 2018: 38-39).

Flooding in the ancient world was a type of judgment, and the ancients always searched for the root cause of their gods' anger? The people acknowledged the unpredictable and petty nature of the gods they served. Their gods were corrupt beings who constantly promoted violence and chaos. For Israel, however, the Genesis flood story offered something different. Presenting the flood story in a radically different way subverted the mission of the gods of the surrounding nations. Walton explains that the biblical interpretation of the flood narrative "constitutes the divine message that carries the authority of the text," adding that events in the Bible were not authoritative in and of themselves but that the interpretation of those events was authoritative. According to Walton, it is "not a matter of what is seen but what the viewer is supposed to see" (18).

In the Genesis flood story, YHWH was not so angry that He decided to destroy all of humanity. After all, He offered to save mankind from the flood judgment by instructing Noah to build an ark. His desire was to restore order from the chaos the nation's gods had wreaked upon the world and to reinitiate relationship with humanity. YHWH's desire was a world filled with peace, harmony, and love under His sovereign rule. "In these flood stories, all that water coming to destroy humanity was often believed to be divine judgment for all of the ways people had made a mess of things. The gods are angry, it was believed, and a flood was their way of clearing the deck to start over" (Bell 2019: 91).

In the *Epic of Gilgamesh*, Gilgamesh is introduced as the legendary ruler of Uruk who, like all kings of the ancient world, desired immortality. This desire led him to make a dangerous journey in search of Utnapishtim—the sole survivor of the Babylonian flood. Utnapishtim revealed how he survived the flood and provided Gilgamesh with the location of a plant that would "renew" his youth. The plant, however, was eaten by a serpent which forced Gilgamesh to return to Uruk without having achieved eternal life.

Like Noah, Utnapishtim was forewarned by the gods that a great flood was coming. He too built a boat and loaded it with precious cargo that included his kin, domesticated and wild animals, and skilled craftsmen. He survived six days while the rest of mankind drowned in the floodwaters. When Utnapishtim's boat finally came to rest on Mount Nimush, he released a dove, a swallow, and a raven—only the raven did not return. Based on these Mesopotamian epics, it becomes clear that immortality was the sole goal of the "ruling" classes. The flood heroes (Atrahasis, Ziusdura or Utnapishtim) all survived the deluge and thus were granted immortality by the gods.

The impulsive, capricious nature of the gods dominated the lives of ancient people. Legend has it that the gods complained endlessly about manual labor before creating humans to serve their needs. They enslaved and oppressed their subjects, forcing them to meet the economic needs of the empire. Since the gods had no regard for human life, the people were stripped of their human dignity and freedom. The gods' primary concern was human overpopulation, so famine, drought, and/or flood were the best options for exercising control. The gods of men were not real, of course, but they did represent the motivations and directives of the movers and shakers of the time. Modern readers understand the world of the gods in a mythological sense. For the ancients, the gods represented the ruling class who functioned largely in a political setting.

For Israel, the flood was seen as a direct result of a lack of righteousness and justice. The judgment of the One True God was directly due to the wicked inclination of the people's hearts—especially their leaders. Most scholars agree that the flood story was written down while Israel was in exile. Israel's covenant breaking had led to their exile, which in turn had led to the degradation of marriage, the destruction of the family, and the inability of the earth to produce enough food. The flood story exemplified *YHWH's* desire to save the righteous and to renew the earth. This was accomplished by re-establishing His eternal covenant, the sign of which was a bow in the sky, and promising never to flood the earth again.

The righteous hero Noah instituted order/rest on the earth by building an ark/temple to preserve his seed. The polluted earth was immersed in the floodwaters so it could be cleansed and purified. The deluge ended the first creation while the ark carried the embryonic second creation into a new era—one of new creation and a rebuilding of the cosmic house.

Water in the ancient world was seen as an agent of judgment. The deluge established the belief that through water the wicked are judged and the righteous are delivered. The righteous ultimately found refuge atop the mountain which represented the inner sanctum of a temple, while the wicked were condemned to the underworld. For Israel looking back at the story of Noah, the flood had reversed *YHWH's* created order. The reappearance of the unrestrained, hostile waters signaled a return to chaos. "The main features of the subsequent divine-river rituals were all found in the judgment of the flood: the direct revelation of the divine verdict, the use of water as the ordeal element, the overpowering of the condemned and the deliverance of the justified, and the entrance of the ark-saved heirs of the new world into the possession of the erstwhile estates of the ungodly" (Kline 1965: 132). The motion of the ark upon the face of the waters, like the Spirit of God hovering over the waters at creation, foreshadowed the coming of light and life.

In Mesopotamia, the accused would cast himself into the river—into the hands of the divine judge. If he emerged from the waters, he was found innocent. If he was overpowered by the river, he was found guilty and condemned to the watery abode of the dead: the netherworld. The threat of death was linked to the raging waters.

She'ol was connected to these hostile waters as a pit located at the foot of the world mountain where judgments were made. King David spoke of *She'ol* in a Psalm for the dedication of the Temple. "*Adonai*, you brought my soul up from *She'ol*. You kept me alive, so I would not go down to the pit" (Ps. 30.4). Many heroes of the Bible overcame the angry waters of chaos, including Moses, Joshua, Jonah, and *Yeshua*. *YHWH* regularly rescued his own from the depths of *She'ol* which was seen as a place of judgment.

Over time, floods became synonymous with invading armies; the seas represented the "noise" of the gentile nations. "Oy! The uproar of many peoples who roar like the roaring of the seas. The rumbling of nations, who rush in like the rumbling of mighty waters! The nations will rush in like the rumbling of many waters, but He will rebuke them..." (Is. 17.12,13a). "You who still the noise of the seas, the noise of the waves, and the tumult of the people" (Ps. 65.8).

The sea was the enemy of order in the ancient world. According to Jon Levenson, its defeat was an essential element in creation. The victorious god won his kingship and the right to a palace of his own. Creation, kingship, and temple form a triad. The containment of the sea is proof of their eternal validity (1985: 108-9).

Pharaoh was compared to a monster in the seas. "You are like a young lion among the nations, And you are like a monster in the seas, Bursting forth in your rivers, Troubling the waters with your feet, And fouling their rivers" (Ezek. 32.2 NKJV).

The oppressive anti-life measures of the nations worked in opposition to the creational order. Egypt came to embody these chaotic forces when it enslaved Israel.

The armies of the king of Assyria were compared to a river that flooded Israel and later Judah. Assyria's conquest of the northern kingdom of Israel took place in 722 BCE against its capital city, Samaria. Twenty years later, the Assyrians came against King Hezekiah of Judah. "... Adonai is bringing on them the waters of the River—mighty and massive—Assyria's king with all his glory! It will rise over all its channels and spill over all its banks. Then it will sweep through Judah, overflow as it passes through, reaching even to the neck" (Is. 8.7-8). "Then the people of a prince who is to come will destroy the city and sanctuary. But his end will come like a flood. Until the end of war that is decreed there will be destruction"(Dan. 9.26b).

The prophet Nahum spoke against Nineveh saying that Adonai is a jealous and avenging God. "But with an overwhelming flood, He will make that place a total ruin" (Nah. 1.8). Political rulers like Pharaoh were likened to the serpent adversary. He, Pharaoh, was the great dragon (crocodile) lying in his rivers (Ezek. 29.3). King Nebuchadnezzar acted as a dragon/serpent when he came against Judah (Jer. 51.34).

According to the book of Revelation, "And the great dragon was thrown down—the ancient serpent, called the devil and Satan, who deceives the whole world... and from out of his mouth, the serpent spewed water like a river after the woman, in order to sweep her away with a flood. The earth came to the aid of the woman. The earth opened its mouth and swallowed the river that the dragon had spewed from its mouth" (Rev. 12.9,15-16). The great dragon mentioned here is most likely Caesar Vespasian, as the Roman army came against Israel during the Jewish Wars to destroy the city of Jerusalem, the monarchy, and the Second Temple.

"Mighty men" are portrayed in battle tales as chaotic waters, attacking and undoing God's creation (Morales 2012:

134 notes). In the combat myth scenario, the warrior god rises up for battle to overcome the seas: Marduk fights against Tiamat, *YHWH* defeats Leviathan, and Ba'al goes against *Yam* (Canaanite god). The purpose of these battles was three-fold: to establish cosmic order, to raise up kingship among the gods, and to lay the foundation for building a temple (Levenson 1985: 152-53). Walton explains that the victor, the divine warrior, first faces adversity and then ascends the sacred mountain to be acclaimed king over the cosmos. God's mastery over the seas is a dominant theme throughout the Bible.

According to Morales, when a temple stood its existence was associated with controlling the forces of chaos or water (Morales 2012: 160). A later re-telling of Noah's ark likely gave hope to the exiles in Babylon that Solomon's temple would be rebuilt. Additionally, Blenkinsopp notes that the climax of the flood story is really the founding of a temple over the source of the floodwaters, and that Israel's version is a cosmogonic victory by *YHWH* that results in building a sanctuary. *Yeshua* declared that those who hear his words and do them will be like a wise man who builds his house on the rock. "And the rain fell and the floods came and the wind blew and beat against that house; and yet it did not fall for its foundation had been built on the rock" (Matt. 2.24).

According to Margaret Barker, Israel saw creation as the Lord's triumph over the primeval waters in that he established dry ground—a place where a temple could be erected. Conflict with the waters/seas, which represent chaos, appears throughout Scripture. God's triumph over the waters meant He defeated His enemies to claim his rightful place as King. Psalm eighty-nine speaks of the triumph of God and His *Davidic* king in conquering the seas: "You rule over the swelling sea. When its waves mount up, you still them. You crushed *Rahav* like a slain one. You scattered your enemies with your mighty arm" (89.10-11). *YHWH* defeated the monster in the sea, Leviathan, the dragon of old, the twisted serpent, the one with seven heads. "I will set his hand over the sea, his right hand over the rivers. He will call to Me: You are my Father, my God and the rock of my salvation. I also will set him as firstborn—the highest of the kings of earth" (Ps. 89.26-28).

As an interesting aside, it's possible those who compiled the Bible wanted to emphasize the significance of the flood in an unusual way. The first letter of the Hebrew Scriptures (Gen. 1.1) is the enlarged Hebrew letter *bet* in *beresheet* (in the beginning). The center letter of the Torah is an enlarged *vav* found in the word *gachon* which means belly (Lev. 11.42), and the final letter of the Torah is a *lamed* which is the last letter in the word Israel (Deut. 34.12). Together, these three letters form the Hebrew word *bul*, which means flood.

CHAPTER TWO

ARCHITECTURE

My Lord, You have been our dwelling
From generation to generation.
Before the mountains were born,
Or You gave birth to the earth and the world,
Even from everlasting to everlasting
You are God!
Psalm 90.1b,2

Mountain ideology is an important key to understanding the mythological world of the Ancient Near East (ANE), and, by extension, the Bible. To the ancients, the sacred cosmic mountain stood at the intersection between Heaven and Earth. Equating temples with mountains was fundamental and ancient Near Eastern texts are replete with this type of imagery. The mountain became a symbol for temples on the basis of architecture, ritual, and rulership. Many events in the New Testament took place atop mountains: *Yeshua* stood or sat on an unnamed mountain for his transfiguration, the commissioning of his apostles, the sermon on the mount, and his resurrection.

Morales stated that Eden's mountain was the archetype for the cosmic mountain (2015: 15). Emphasizing this same point, Jon Levenson explained why temples were built on mountains: "The Temple offers the person who enters it to worship an opportunity to rise from a fallen world, to partake of the Garden of Eden" (1984: 298). The cosmic mountain can be found throughout Scripture especially in key moments in Israel's history. "From the beginning, the garden Paradise of Eden was located on the Mountain of God. Its summit was God's inner chamber—the site of the Holy of Holies. The book of *Jubilees* points to Eden as a cosmic mountain that the flood waters were unable to overcome" (Fishbane 1998: 111-120). "And [Noah] knew that Eden was the Holy of Holies and the dwelling of *YHWH*" (*Jubilees* 8.19).

The mountain was always the ultimate destination. "The mountain is the goal of pilgrimage of the final rest after escape from the dominion of evil. The mountain of God in the beginning has become the mountain of God at the end" (Clifford 1984: 123). The pilgrim progresses through levels that involve great danger and difficulty, starting at the lowest realm and climbing to the highest heavens—Paradise. In ANE thought, however, only the gods, heroes of old, or the purified souls of the deceased overcame the challenges in ascending (Wiercinski 1976: 200). At his crucifixion, *Yeshua* told the thief, "Amen, I tell you, today you shall be with Me in Paradise" (Luke 23.43). *Yeshua* promised the thief that he too would ascend to serve as gardener in the Edenic sanctuary.

In ancient literature, mountains were generally pictured in groups of three, not arranged across the horizon, but rather stacked three high, one on top of the other reaching into the heavens (Parry 1994: 136). Enoch described Paradise as mountains—the middle of which reached into heaven like the throne of God with its top as lapis lazuli and fire (1 *Enoch* 18.6-12,24). "This high mountain that you saw, whose peak is like the throne of God, is the seat where the Great Holy One, the Lord of glory, the King of eternity will sit when he descends to visit the earth in goodness" (25:3). (The Book of *Enoch* is an important work for its historical and religious development in Judaism dating from 200 BCE to 100 CE. It is part of the Pseudepigrapha:

Jewish writings whose authors used a pseudonym.)

In Ephrem's *Hymns of Paradise* (mid 4th Century CE), Paradise is described as a mountain divided into three levels with the lowest for penitents, the next for the righteous, and the highest for the triumphant (Eden being the cosmic mountain par excellence) (Quoted in Barker 2008: 99). The imagery of three mountains as a kind of successive ascension into heaven may explain Paul's cryptic comment about knowing a man who was caught up in the third heaven (2 Cor. 12.2). Perhaps Paul was speaking of the triumphant one who will experience Paradise at the highest level, which was symbolic of entering heaven.

Mountains were the first fixed element born of the primeval waters. Eden's mountain originated from the waters of creation. Ararat's mountain rose out of the raging waters of the flood. Sinai's mountain stood as the bulwark against the chaos of *Yam Suph*, the Sea of Reeds. Zion emerged as chief among mountains after Israel crossed the Jordan River to the promised land. Raging rivers, foam-tossed seas, and chaotic waters came to symbolize the gentile nations as well as Israel's exile into those nations. The mountain served as a hedge of protection for Israel against her enemies.

The mountain's subterranean layer was seen as the underworld (also called "the deep"). This unseen realm of the dead was located at the lowest point of existence and was referred to as the depths of *she'ol*, a place of darkness, the pit, or the grave.

The mountain peak by contrast represented new life and new birth, and for the ancients it represented the oracle of the gods. For Israel, the peak was at the summit where the Divine King sat enthroned in His royal sanctuary. At the summit was the Foundation Stone where the Ark of the Covenant, containing the holy oracles of *YHWH*, was located.

The prophet Ezekiel, contemporary of Jeremiah, was exiled to Babylon before Jerusalem fell and the Temple was destroyed (586 BCE). Though he continuously warned of the coming destruction by King Nebuchadnezzar of Babylon, Ezekiel also encouraged the people by heralding the future restoration of the Temple (Ezek. 40-48). Ezekiel pictured Israel's return to the land as dry bones coming to life (37) which served as a metaphor for Israel's rebirth. Ezekiel reminded the people that they should look ahead to rebuilding the Temple which would again house the glory of God. He told them—that they would establish it again as the center or navel of the Earth on the mountains of Zion. A rebuilt Temple signified that the restoration of Eden had come, even amidst the greatest of all national tragedies—exile in Babylon.

King of the Hill

> The kings of earth set themselves up and rulers conspire together against *Adonai* and against His Anointed one. I have set up My king upon Zion, My holy mountain.
>
> PSALM 2.2,6

The ANE world saw kingship as an invention of the gods which came down from heaven. Cosmic order depended on which king was chosen. The right king assured that the proper gods were in control of the universe. "Once kingship had been invented, this institution wrapped itself so securely and intimately around the concept of power and statehood that a state without a king was an anomaly" (Podany 2014: 27).

The king's induction included a ritual ascent on the day of his inauguration. He was transformed into a divine being who ascended to heaven. "When the royal candidate sat down on the throne in the temple, this meant nothing less than his ascent to the sacred mountain and adoption among the gods" (Lang 2002: 19-21). The king's enthronement was a "heavenly" act that transformed him from a mere mortal into a god.

Kings enjoyed special access to the gods—approaching them through a series of rituals that involved "entering the sanctuary, ascending the temple tower, and raising hands to heaven in a gesture affirming contact had been achieved" (Lang quoted in Morales 2012: 283). This may explain why Aaron and Hur placed a stone under Moses and supported his raised hands (Ex. 17.11-12). Perhaps the three ascending to the "top of the hill" and Moses "sitting" on the stone was part of a kingship ritual. And perhaps holding up Moses' hands affirmed contact had been achieved with *YHWH* resulting in Joshua's defeat of the Amalekites (8-15). After all, a king's main responsibility was to militarily defeat his god's enemies and bring peace and prosperity to his subjects.

Some view Moses' ascension into Sinai's cloud-filled Paradise as a picture of a new Adam. It has also been suggested that Noah, whose name means rest, represents a new Adam figure with the ark coming to "rest" on Mt. Ararat. In the ancient world, rest implied that a king had defeated his enemies, took the throne and established justice and righteousness for his subjects. God "resting" Adam in Eden was part of this kingship ritual. Noah and Moses both built sanctuaries—the ark and the tabernacle. Building was the responsibility of ancient kings as the way of maintaining creational order. Morales said of Moses and Noah, that in passing through the waters to approach the deity on top of the mountain, they stood in the footprints of Adam (Morales 2012: 216).

"Moses ascending corresponded to a typical Mesopotamian royal pattern in which the king ascends to God, is given the tablets of destiny, and gets a special commission as a Messenger or Apostle of God" (Widengren 1957: 17-18). Dozeman agrees with this assessment and considers Exodus nineteen as "the enthronement of God on the mountain" (2009: 456). Moses' repeated trips up and down the mountain related the two worlds, Heaven and Earth, in the setting of the divine mountain" (433-434). Widengren sees Moses as a type of *Davidic* king ruling from Mt. Zion in Jerusalem; his ascending the mountain equates to a coronation. Enthronement and kingship were connected to the mountain's summit where the central sanctuary was located. Adam on Eden, Noah on Ararat, Moses on Sinai, David on Zion, and *Yeshua* on the Mt. of Olives match the kingship pattern. They all ascended the mountain in king-like fashion to enter the Presence of their God.

Solomon's enthronement followed a similar pattern: He first descended to the Gihon Spring for his anointing and then ascended Zion's mountain to sit on the throne. "Zadok the *Kohen* and Nathan the Prophet have anointed him king at Gihon. From there they have come up rejoicing so that the city is in an uproar... also Solomon has taken his seat on the royal throne" (I Kings 1.45-46). The Gihon, located beneath the City of David, originated from an underground cave and provided drinking water for the city's residents. In the creation account, the Gihon was one of four rivers that watered the garden in Eden (Gen. 2.10). The cosmic mountain emerged from those waters to become the throne of the divine ruler.

This ascension theme permeates the Psalms: "Who may ascend the mountain of *Adonai*? Who may stand in His Holy Place? One with clean hands and a pure heart, who has not lifted his soul in vain, nor sworn deceitfully" (Ps. 24.3,4 NKJV). The Psalms lay out the protocol for worshipping Israel's God—worship being the *telos* or goal of creation—with order being maintained through the king's enthronement and his future rulings and decrees.

✡ ✡ ✡

Sargon I of the Akkadian empire was the first worldwide ruler (24th century BCE). His name means Legitimate King, and he forged his kingdom by conquering the Sumerian city-states. Sargon embarked on a series of military campaigns to subjugate the entire Fertile Crescent. Through his relentless and brutal attacks, he gobbled up territory from Mesopotamia to the Levant and from the Mediterranean Sea to the Persian Gulf. City after city fell to Sargon followed by his plundering of resources. Throughout the empire, he replaced local rulers with his own officials. The people were forced to pay tribute with most of the proceeds going to build his capital city, Akkad (Gen. 10.10)—the seat of the empire. Located on the western bank of the Euphrates, Akkad set the standard for centralized government as Sargon made significant improvements over the organization of the earlier city-states.

Sargon set the stage for upcoming empires. And like all good tyrants, he censored the truth and rewrote a flattering history of his heroic deeds for future kings to emulate (Podany 2014: 38-43). Mesopotamian, Assyrian, and Babylonian rulers followed in his footsteps, seeing themselves as the heir apparent of Sargon's first world empire. These world rulers further expanded their empires into vast urban complexes.

Sargon maintained control by securing land and sea trade routes and embarking on a path of global domination. His vast road construction benefited trading partners including those from the silver mines of Anatolia, the lapis lazuli mines of what is now Afghanistan, and the forests of Lebanon which were a source of the great cedars. Sargon's empire was an economic and political powerhouse. As he continued building massive fortresses for wheat production, his empire developed into the world's breadbasket. As it has often been said, he who controls the food supply controls the world. In an interesting aside, the Akkadian empire designed the world's first postal service using clay tablets inscribed in cuneiform Akkadian script. These tablets were wrapped in outer clay envelopes and marked with the name and address of the recipient along with the seal of the sender.

A king "stood in" as his god's living representative on Earth. When a king launched a military campaign, a statue was erected in his absence that bore the face of his god. The image was carved from wood and overlaid with gold or silver, or it was chiseled from stone and fire gilded with precious metals. This idol was placed in the temple where the king's subjects could worship his image.

King Manasseh of Judah placed a carved image in the House of God (2 Chr. 33.7) in violation of the Lord's command not to worship foreign gods or graven images. He made an Asherah, an image called the abomination of the nations, in order to worship the host of heaven. Manasseh continually led his people astray causing them to do evil in the sight of the Lord. In response, God sent the Assyrian army, likely under King Esarhaddon (the youngest son of Sennacherib), to forcibly remove Manasseh. They led him away with nose hooks and chains. According to the Biblical text, Manasseh later repented and was allowed to return to Jerusalem where he restored worship of the One True God.

Daniel tells of the King of the North rising up and profaning the Temple, stopping the daily offerings, and setting up the abomination of desolation—an image of the king with the face of his god that the people could worship in his absence. The king had set off on a number of military campaigns, invaded lands, and plundered the riches of Egypt (Dan. 11.31-45).

Isaiah (44) addresses the folly of erecting these idols. Isaiah's words warn Israel's kings against making images of themselves like the ANE rulers did. God cautioned against shaping the image into the figure of man that would sit in its shrine. God warned Israel against falling down and worshipping the idol. The "image of the beast" in Revelation (13) picks up on this theme with the living image being a representation of both the god and his king.

Chapter after chapter in the Bible deals with kingship and empire building from a political perspective. The book of Isaiah shows Israel living among a series of foreign kings and their empires including the Assyrians, the Babylonians, and the Persians. Kings such as Sennacherib and Tiglath Pileser III of Assyria and Nebuchadnezzar of Babylon were used by God as instruments of judgment against Israel. They were often likened to a rod of God's anger sent against an ungodly nation. For the people living in an imperialistic setting, there was hope in *YHWH's* message that one day He would rule from Zion's mountain and that all nations would travel there to seek His glory. On that day, the mountains of Zion would be the hub of an international kingdom.

Ancient rulers saw their cities as the center of the civilized world with the outside world being a hostile, untamed territory. Within the walled enclosures of the nation's temple were well-watered gardens along with towers to contain the king's vast array of wild animals. Although horticulture was the king's primary vocation, hunting was the ideal sport. Subduing outside threats from savage animals, beasts, and undomesticated wildlife was the responsibility of the king. Beasts later became synonymous with rulers of foreign empires who were seen as the number one external threat to the kingdom. It became the king's duty to rid the land of these dangerous interlopers in order to have control over his nation.

The ultimate sign of the king's royal authority was in his ability to subdue the world's most powerful animal, namely the lion. Hunting lions showcased the king's ability to shepherd and protect his flock. The first evidence that hunting was a symbol of royal authority appeared in the city of Uruk in Mesopotamia. A stele (c. 3400 BCE) showed a leader displaying his power by battling a lion during the hunt. In ancient Assyria, the lion hunt displayed the king's prowess and proved his bravery and royal authority. Hunting was inextricably tied to kingship. It was a royal function that established the king's power along with the vitality of the state. A successful hunt showed the gods' favor upon the kingdom.

Nimrod, great-grandson of Noah, was the first hunter named in the Bible. He became mighty in the land and a mighty hunter before the Lord. "The beginning of his kingdom included Babel, Erech [likely Uruk], Akkad and Calneh...from that land he went out to Assyria and built Nineveh" (Gen. 10.9,10). Extra Biblical tradition associates Nimrod with the Tower of Babel. Scholars have so far been unable to match Nimrod with any historical figure. Some suggest Nimrod may be a title or that the name may represent a specific people group in Mesopotamia. Some modern scholars suggest his placement in the Bible is of Babylonian origin related to Israel's captivity. Many possibilities have been suggested for Nimrod: Gilgamesh, Marduk, Sargon I of Assyria, or the later Sennacherib of Assyria. If the Bible's Tower of Babel is a reworking of an ancient myth, then King Nebuchadnezzar would be the most likely choice.

"The name 'Nimrod' from *marad*, 'We will revolt,' points to some violent resistance to God... Nimrod as a mighty hunter founded a powerful kingdom...the result of his strength in hunting, so that hunting was intimately connected with the establishing of the kingdom. If the expression 'a mighty hunter' relates primarily to hunting in the literal sense, we must add to the literal meaning the figurative signification of a 'hunter of men' [a trapper of men by stratagem and force]; Nimrod the hunter became a tyrant, a powerful hunter of men" (Keil and Delitzsch 1975: 165).

Josephus said of Nimrod: "[he] gradually changed the government into tyranny—seeing no other way of turning men from the fear of God but to bring them into a constant dependence upon his own power" (*Antiquities of the Jews*, I: iv: 2). Kings as hunters had more to do with controlling men, bringing them into submission, and removing their freedom. By exercising tyranny, a king would enslave his subjects and force them to depend on the king's provision. Israel experienced this kind of tyranny in Egypt. Pharaoh forced the Children of Israel to build Egyptian cities, including infra-structure, and to labor as slaves in the fields for food production. In the Bible, Egypt was just the first of many foreign nations to subjugate and oppress Israel.

Empire: Mountain And Beast

In the ANE world, cosmic mountains were associated with permanence, stability, and strength. On the summit, a sacred sanctuary housed the seat of government—a throne from which the king ruled the empire. Under the authority of his god, the king officiated alongside his divine council called the host of heaven. He oversaw the empire's judicial, commercial, religious, and economic functions. One of the most important responsibilities of the governing body was to manage food production. Most residents worked for the administrative state as laborers: farmers, herdsmen, artisans, etc. The ruling elites, on the other hand, planned out military campaigns in order to expand the empire.

The book of Daniel tells the story of "world empire" in dramatic fashion. From the Babylonians to the Roman Empire, the gentile nations repeatedly oppressed Israel. Daniel focuses mostly on King Nebuchadnezzar II and the Babylonian empire (605-562 BCE). This is the empire that took Israel into captivity. The book is set during Israel's exile with some events occurring later in history.

Modern scholars think Daniel is largely fictional but that it is based on Israel's experience in captivity. It was likely written in the Second Century BCE—a period in which apocalyptic literature flourished. This literary genre describes historical events using cosmic type language. Though sensational in its predictions, it does not actually deal with an end of the world scenario. Second Temple Judaism never viewed the world through an "end times" prism. Rather, the cataclysmic language describes the consequences of Israel's breaking covenant with *YHWH* which resulted in the destruction of the Temple and the end of the monarchy.

Daniel covers the highs and lows of Jewish history following the Babylonian exile. It records a history of trouble and tribulation for the people of God who were continuously subjected to foreign rule under the gentile nations: the Babylonians, Persians, Greeks, and Romans. Its central message is that God rules history and will ultimately vindicate His people. He will restore the *Davidic* monarchy by returning Israel's rightful king to the throne on Zion.

Daniel asked to interpret King Nebuchadnezzar's dream in which a dazzling image appeared with a head of gold, arms of silver, belly and thighs of bronze, legs of iron, and feet of iron and clay. A stone cut from a mountain struck the feet of the statue, causing it to fall and crumble leaving no trace behind. "Then the stone that struck the image became a great mountain and filled the whole earth" (Dan. 2.35b). Though Daniel identified each part of the statue as a succeeding world empire, there is plenty of debate over these empires' specific identities. Modern scholars connect the head with Babylon, the arms with the Medes, the thighs with Persia, and the legs and feet with the Seleucids and Ptolemies. (Christian eschatologists identify the head with Babylon, the arms with the Medes and Persians, the belly and thighs with Greece, and the legs and feet with Rome). In the king's dream, the stone became a great (cosmic) mountain that filled the earth. This mountain represented the restored Kingdom of Judah whose center was Jerusalem.

The sacredness of the holy mountain passed to the sacredness of the Holy Temple. The qualities of the mountain, order and definition, were qualities inextricably linked to the sanctuary. Just as the mountain signified victory over the waters of chaos at creation, so too, the rebuilt Temple represented God's victory over His enemies: the surrounding gentile nations. The "newborn" king, represented in King Nebuchadnezzar's dream by the stone cut from the mountain, would be seated on the throne, to rule and reign over the world from Zion. King Nebuchadnezzar's dream was about a new creation event: the king enthroned in the sanctuary. It was also a reminder to Israel of the birth of Eden's mountain at creation. The message was straightforward: *YHWH's* kingdom would never be destroyed, and the royal dynasty of David would forever rule the nations. The enthronement of Israel's king on the earth would be seen as a highly subversive act to the gentile rulers. The birth of *Yeshua* the Messiah, the newborn King of Israel, would further subvert the political order of King Herod, the Temple leadership, and Rome.

The Medo-Persian empire was represented by the bronze belly and thighs. Ezekiel's highly detailed descriptions of the rebuilt Temple (40-48) begins with a man "whose appearance was like bronze" (Ezek. 40.3). This is perhaps the figure of Cyrus the Great of Persia (the Achaemenid Empire was founded by Cyrus in 539 BCE) who issued a decree to allow the Jews to return from Babylon to rebuild the Temple: a truly subversive response in the face of the Babylonians. "Now in the first year of King Cyrus of Persia... *Adonai* stirred up the spirit of King Cyrus of Persia so that he sent a proclamation throughout all his kingdom... thus says King Cyrus of Persia: *Adonai*, the God of heaven, has given me all the kingdoms of the earth. He has appointed me to build Him a House in Jerusalem, which is in Judah" (2 Chr. 36.22,23a). "In visions God brought me to the land of Israel and set me down upon a very high mountain" (Ezek. 40.2). Mountain imagery dominates the narrative: A "cosmic" mountain called Zion will be the foundation for a new creation Temple, and the rightful king will be enthroned to rule over the nations.

Cosmic mountain theology helps explain *Yeshua's* words concerning faith and moving a mountain: "Amen, I tell you, if someone says to this mountain, 'Be taken up and thrown into the sea,' and does not doubt in his heart but trusts that what he says is happening, so shall it be for him" (Mark 11.23). The context of this chapter is key to understanding *Yeshua's* meaning here. *Yeshua*, after having arrived at the summit of the Mt. of Olives, sent two disciples into a village to bring him a colt that had never been sat upon. It is unclear which village the disciples went to, but Bethphage seems the likely candidate. Bethphage, or *Beit Pagey*, "House of Unripe Figs," was home to the priestly class who serviced the altar of the red heifer atop the Mt. of Olives. In Scripture, bad or immature figs allude to Israel's corrupt leadership (Jer. 24).

In this scene from Mark, the crowd responds to *Yeshua* on the colt with an acclamation to the king: "Blessed is the coming kingdom of our father David! Hosanna in the highest" (11.10). Next, *Yeshua* enters the city of Jerusalem and the Temple complex where he drives out the money changers and rails against the ruling priests and scribes for making the Temple a den of thieves. A little while later, the disciples observe a fig tree shriveled from the roots. It is at this point that *Yeshua* speaks of a mountain being cast into the sea. To be sure, he is not speaking in literal terms of imagining or conjuring up enough faith to move a mountain range from one location to another. Here he is speaking metaphorically. He is excoriating a corrupt leadership who are indulging in acts of bribery and extortion from the Temple itself. *Yeshua* assures his disciples a new Kingdom is at hand, one based not on power and control but on covenantal faith with *YHWH*. This Kingdom will subvert power and replace the current ruling elites running the Temple. He promises his disciples a kingdom that will bring order instead of the chaos that human rulers have produced because of their covetousness, arrogance, and greed.

Throughout the book of Matthew, *Yeshua* often denounces the Temple leadership. Written to Jewish believers, the book promotes the idea of Jews and non-Jews as legitimate heirs of the Kingdom. We see *Yeshua*, once again, subverting the current power structure by telling his disciples that with covenantal faith this temple/mountain structure will be cast into the sea—upended and lost to the nations. "God is our refuge and strength, an ever-present help in trouble. Therefore we will not fear, though the earth be removed, though the mountains topple into the heart of the seas. Nations are in an uproar, kingdoms totter, He utters His voice, the earth melts! *Adonai* is with us. The God of Jacob is our stronghold" (Ps. 46.2-3,7-8).

At the time of King Belshazzar of Babylon, Daniel dreamed of four huge beasts coming out of the sea: a lion, a bear, a leopard, and a terrifying beast with ten horns that waged war against the saints. The beasts represented the gentile nations and their kings. Just as beasts hunt their prey, these kings would hunt men. Beasts coming up out of the sea were seen as a tool of judgment in ANE culture.

Chief among the beasts was the serpent (referred to as satan, the devil, or the great sea monster of the deep), a creature of chaos who preyed upon God's elect. In his article *Leviathan: Sea Dragon of Chaos* Brian Godawa explains that "[i]n ANE religious mythologies, the sea and the sea dragon were symbols of chaos that needed to be overcome to bring order to the universe, or in more exact terms, the political world order of the myth's originating culture." For the ancients, this was *the* divine struggle: overcoming chaos. Order was the highest value in their world, and the king brought political order when he defeated his enemies militarily. Destroying "chaos creatures" signified the kingdom could return to a state of peace, rest, and tranquility.

The dragon was the Pharaoh who created chaos for Israel. "In that day, *Adonai* will punish Leviathan, the fleeing serpent with His fierce, great, strong, sword, Leviathan the twisting serpent! He will slay the dragon in the sea" (Is. 27.1). It is unclear whether this reference to a sea monster is referring to the ruler of Egypt, Assyria, or Babylon. Regardless, political power rested in the Leviathan: the adversary, the devil, or the ruler of darkness. The battle against chaos, though described in cosmic terms, should be understood in a political context. Overcoming the sea was likened to overcoming a political entity and the sea monster who was its ruler.

The Bible's depiction of Pharaoh drowning in the deep of *Yam Suph* (along with his chariot army) is the telling of a major military defeat in a way that is likened to a cosmic battle. Israel won that victory by the hand of *YHWH* and so passed through the sea on dry ground. Dry ground appeared on the third day of the creation week as the primordial hillock or mountain: the bulwark against chaos. Crossing the sea on dry ground was a re-creation event in which Israel's enemies were defeated. This was a subversive response to world power.

In Ephesians (6.10-17), Paul describes how the community can subvert world power by wearing God's armor (Is. 59.17) and proclaiming the truth of the Gospel which includes worship and prayer. Roman power was centered in Ephesus, a Greek colony on the eastern coast of Asia Minor. The people of Ephesus worshipped the great mother goddess Artemis (Roman goddess Diana), the goddess of hunting, wild animals, and fertility (Acts 19). Her magnificent temple was one of the seven wonders of the ancient world. As a cosmopolitan center, it was an important trading hub in Asia and home to leading political thinkers and intellectuals.

Paul describes putting on the whole armor of God. Through his description, he is likely alluding to the Roman soldiers in Asia Minor as there was a small garrison in Ephesus. The sword, compared to the Word of God, was being used as an offensive weapon to advance and reclaim lost territory from the enemy. "Put on the full armor of God so that you are able to stand against the schemes of the devil" [the current ruler over the Roman Empire]. For our struggle is not against flesh and blood, but against the rulers, against the powers, against the worldly forces of this darkness and against spiritual forces of wickedness in heavenly places" (Eph. 6.11-12). Our battle is not against flesh and blood humanity but against the political elites and ruling classes of the day. Clearly, wearing the armor and advancing against those ruling authorities in worship and prayer was and is a subversive act.

Ziggurats And Mountains

In Mesopotamia, the ancients built sanctuaries for their gods atop man-made mountains called ziggurats. With no natural elevation in the region, the ziggurat functioned as the perfect platform for their sacred shrines. According to Morales, pyramids and ziggurats were architectural representations of the cosmic mountain (2015: 61). From the word *zagaru* or *zigguratu* meaning "to be high or lifted up," the ziggurat was a temple tower with its four sides rising up from a man-made platform in the shape of a square or rectangle. Mesopotamian seals featured a god emerging from a cosmic mountain. This supports the idea of a ziggurat as both a mountain and an impressive architectural achievement of the ANE world.

The ziggurat consisted of a monumental staircase leading up to a first level gate with a second terrace supporting the platform upon which either a temple or successive terraces were built. The ziggurat contained no internal chambers but was filled with dirt. The exterior was covered with sun-dried mud bricks since stones in the alluvial plain were in short supply. Local bitumen provided the mortar. The terracing enabled access to those ascending the summit where the god resided. The ziggurat's architectural design confirmed a connection between the heavens and the earth and between the god and mankind. Vertically, it connected earth and sky; horizontally, it connected the four cardinal directions. Though an artificial mound, the ziggurat created a natural transition between the sacred mountain and man-made stage towers.

Babylonian ziggurats had names such as "Mountain of the House" or "House of the Mountain of all Lands." The Etemenanki ziggurat, meaning "House of the Foundation of Heaven on Earth," was dedicated to the Babylonian patron god Marduk. Every ancient city had a ziggurat dedicated to their particular god. The great temple of Marduk was an example of this stage-tower construction which the Babylonians inherited from the earlier Sumerians (Morales 2012: 9-10). Etemenanki's design was a familiar stepped pyramid with horizontal measurements at the base corresponding to the total vertical rise (Crawford 2013: 9).

Etemenanki was likely built by Hammurabi, an earlier Babylonian king (1792 to 1750 BCE). King Nebuchadnezzar was responsible for enlarging it. The typical Babylonian ziggurat of the late third millennium BCE was a seven-tiered stepped structure (Haupt 1927: 10), although some were three, nine, or twelve levels. The seven tiers related to the seven planetary and zodiacal regions of the heavens.

Ziggurats were built to overcome flooding from Mesopotamia's two rivers: the Tigris and Euphrates. "The design of the ziggurat is interesting on its own terms, as it was elevated to preserve the shrine from flooding" (Wright 1944: 66-67). Mythologically speaking, ziggurats were founded upon the apsu: fresh water from underground aquifers referred to as the primeval sea. The mythological ziggurat was the primeval mound upon which the universe was created; it rose up from the alluvial plains to become a great, artificial mountain. It functioned as a bulwark against flooding.

"In the myths of Mesopotamia, Marduk triumphed over the forces of chaos to establish the ordered creation, and his triumph was marked and sealed by erecting his great temple on the ziggurat, a massive artificial mountain" (Barker 2008: 63).

According to the Babylonian creation epic, *Enuma Elish*, the god Marduk had to defend the other gods against the diabolical sea monster Tiamat, who represented the oceans' salt water (Some scholars think Tiamat is a cognate of Scripture's *tehom*: the deep). Tiamat was split in two by Marduk in order to create heaven and earth from her body and the Tigris and Euphrates rivers from her eyes.

Most modern scholars associate the legendary Tower of Babel with a ziggurat: a tower whose top reached into heaven (Gen. 11). Some identify it with Etemenanki which was located in the city of Babylon. The ziggurat's terraced design enabled the gods to descend from their heavenly perch. "*Adonai* came down from heaven to see the city and the tower the sons of man had built"(5).

Some scholars suggest the Tower of Babel story was tied in some way to Israel's captivity in Babylon. And God said, "Let us go down and confuse their language there, so that they will not understand each other's language… that is why it is named Babel, because *Adonai* confused the languages of the entire world there, and from there *Adonai* scattered them over the face of the entire world" (7-9). The reference to God confusing the people's languages could refer to Israel's Hebrew language being replaced with Aramaic, the lingua franca of the sixth century BCE. For Israel, living in exile meant not only losing their language but also their identity—the two things that unified them economically, politically, socially, and religiously. Being absorbed into a foreign land presented many problems, not the least of which was the confusion caused by the language barrier.

According to Van Oudtshoorn's article *Mything the Point*, the Tower of Babel should not be read as an historical account concerning the origin of different nations and languages, but rather it should be understood as folklore in relation to the Babylonian ziggurat. Instead of inferring an impressive technological feat by which humanity could reach heaven, it should be seen as being so small that God came down to have a closer look. Van Oudtshoorn also sees the story as an attempt to de-construct the idea of humans trying to become like God (2015: 1-19).

Dr. Andrew George, expert in Babylonian languages and culture of the Near and Middle East, believes the tower account was written during the Babylonian exile. He thinks the Jews in exile actually witnessed the tower's construction while in captivity and it reminded them of the loss of their mountain sanctuary in Zion. They may have seen the tower as a symbol of oppression: a large, looming show of strength constructed by their foreign captors. In this way it would have reaffirmed their desire to return to the land of Israel, to rebuild the Temple on Zion's mountain, and to restore their own national identity.

Holloway sees the Tower of Babel story as a polemic against the ziggurat as a religious symbol "well-nigh universal to Mesopotamian civilization." He believes "[t]he change in the deluge account's ark symbolism from that of cosmic ziggurat to cosmic Solomonic temple was a symbol as peculiar to Judah as one could hope to find." He goes on to say that the deluge of Genesis and the *Epic of Gilgamesh* share a typical ANE context of temple ideology with the ark representing a temple (1991: 349,352).

The tower story suggests that reconstructing the surrounding nations' myths opened the way for Israel to align herself with God's revelation of Himself. It also opened up an avenue to make sense of the exile. Israel had reaped the consequences of her disobedience—most notably the loss of the Presence of God. This is the central catastrophe in the biblical story. The loss of His Presence is later satisfied on Sinai's mountain when Moses receives the blueprint for building the Tabernacle in the wilderness. This seems a fitting resolution to the confusion and scattering in the tower story. Israel's loss is further resolved when Cyrus the Great issues a decree releasing Israel from exile allowing her to return to Zion to rebuild Solomon's Temple which had been destroyed by King Nebuchadnezzar.

Ark And Ziggurat

Some scholars suggest the flood story is a reworking of the story of the Babylonian exile. Israel's exile was symbolic of being swept away by a flood into the nations, thereby losing her identity. Noah's ark was the bulwark against the world's chaos; it was how Noah's family survived. It provided a place for the Presence of God and preserved Noah's future seed. The same would be true for the nation of Israel. Israel's rebuilt Temple would preserve the nation, allow for the return of the Divine Presence, and restore the dynasty of King David after the tragedy of the exile. Fishbane finds a typological association between the flood narrative and the exile: "The ancient covenant of Noah and his descendants will be recapitulated in the post exilic period" (1985: 374). Both events saw the wrath of God manifested; both ended with His divine promise of a continuing seed to restore and maintain the nation: Ham, Shem, and Japheth in the case of Noah, and Zerubbabel in the case of Israel.

Noah and the flood story also share similarities with the *Epic of Gilgamesh*. This epic poem from ancient Mesopotamia is a literary history of King Gilgamesh of Uruk (Erech, Gen. 10.10) that dates from the Third Dynasty of Ur (c. 2100 BCE). Tales of Gilgamesh, the warrior-king of Uruk, go back to the Sumerian period. Historical evidence for Gilgamesh's existence was discovered in ancient inscriptions that credit him with building the great walls of Uruk (modern day Warka, Iraq). Other references can be found in the Sumerian King List which features similar legends around the time of Gilgamesh's reign.

In the poem, King Gilgamesh sought out the flood hero, Utnapishtim, in order to discover the key to immortality. Utnapishtim is introduced in Tablet XI in the standard version of the Babylonian *Epic of Gilgamesh*. He builds an ark, saves his family from the flood, and survives a catastrophic destruction.

Morales suggests the Gilgamesh epic contains many facets of temple ideology. "The ark representing a ziggurat makes it likely that the deluge narrative was authored and understood within the matrix of ANE temple theology" (2012: 151). Holloway thinks both the deluge of Genesis and the *Epic of Gilgamesh* share a typical ANE context of temple ideology with the ark representing a temple (1991: 349-352). In *Gilgamesh XI 95*, the ark is called *Ekallu*. This is a common Akkadian word for a palace or temple, but it is never used of a seagoing vessel. According to John Lundquist, the ark was like a temple providing a divinely appointed haven of safety.

The author of the *Epic of Gilgamesh* describes Utnapishtim's ark as a floating ziggurat measuring 120 cubits in length, width, and height to form a giant cube that was divided into seven horizontal levels. "The ark in Gilgamesh was conceptualized along the lines of a ziggurat" (Holloway 1991: 329). Noah's rectangular ark was thirty cubits high, fifty cubits wide, and three hundred cubits long. It was divided into three levels with a door on the side. According to Gordon Wenham, neither of these boat dimensions accord with ancient nautical construction. Wenham observed that the dimensions of Noah's ark were proportional with the wilderness Tabernacle courtyard area—the surface area of the ark being three times that of much the courtyard (1987: 173).

Holloway says the mythological ark of Utnapishtim was intended to represent a ziggurat (1991: 338). The ark was conceived along the lines of an ideal ziggurat rising in seven stages. Both ziggurat and flood vessel are offshoots of an idealized vision of the cosmos. Many scholars see Utnapishtim's seven-storied ark as having cosmological significance in that it represented a seven-tiered view of the universe. Crawford suggests the ark is reflective of the cosmos because of its connection to the ziggurat.

British archaeologist Mallowan also equates the ark of Utnapishtim with a seven-stage ziggurat and suggests "[t] he narrator had in mind a floating ziggurat and imagined one—always a refuge in time of flood—as sailing over the vast inland sea" (1964: 65). *Gilgamesh XI* contains clues to the ziggurat's identity saying the dimensions of the ark support a temple complex. Etemenanki, the great ziggurat of Babylon, was also of equal height, length, and width. In the *Epic of Gilgamesh*, the flood vessel is exactly the dimensions of the ziggurat of Babylon.

John Lundquist explains the blueprint and measurements for the ark were revealed by the god Ea who saved humanity by warning his servant Utnapishtim of the impending flood. Utnapishtim was told to build a boat whose sides were equal and whose roof was like the apsu because the gods were set to bring a deluge (Morales 2012: 160). According to Holloway, this met the criteria for the "sacral locus of all ziggurats—founded upon the apsu" (1991: 329). Apsu encompasses the world's fresh waters such as underground aquifers, lakes, and springs. In mythology, it refers to the primeval sea.

Modern scholars connect the ark to the cosmic mountain seeing a miniature cosmos and a moving tabernacle, not a boat. From this perspective, Noah's ark is regarded as a house, not a ship. Lundquist explains these two flood boats are best seen as products of ANE temple ideology. They are best expressed as ideals of design, function, and mythology (Holloway 1991: 329). The "[c]lose affiliation of these flood myths with cosmogony bring flood vessel and sacred architecture closer together by definition. The relationship between ark and temple runs deeper than linguistic and structural parallels" (Crawford 2013: 11). Morales further clarifies this vessel had no sails, no rudder, and therefore was not a ship (2015: 59).

In the Gilgamesh epic, a floating vessel appears to be shaped in seven stages like a ziggurat. It represents the cosmos in miniature and serves as a substitute refuge while the cosmos is being cleansed. A temple can stand in for a floating vessel in a mythic narrative (Crawford 2013: 19). Fishbane says as a "cosmos in miniature, the ark providentially survives the universal destruction so that its inhabitants can serve as the nucleus for a renewed world" (1979: 30). "The deluge narrative is not an end but rather the ideological foundation upon which solemn temples, lofty palaces, and entire societies were built" (Pleins 2003: 123).

Noah's ark has been called the "carrier of the cosmos" (4 *Maccabees* 15:31-32) and is seen as the cosmic bridge between creation and re-creation. Morales points to the Tabernacle and the ark as mobile sanctuaries with the Tabernacle also representing a mobile Mt. Sinai. He further explains, "[the] ark moves vertically over water ascending to the mountaintop, the tabernacle moves horizontally over land ascending to the promised land" (2015: 94).

Noah's three-tiered cosmic mountain represented heaven, earth, and the underworld (seas) with the highest level being a symbol of heaven. Josephus spoke of the Holy of Holies as the heavens, the holy place as the earth, and the courtyard as the *tehom* or the deep. Paul boasted on behalf of a man who had seen visions and revelations of the Lord in the third heaven: "I know a man in Christ who fourteen years ago... such a man was caught up to the third heaven. I know such a man—he was caught up into Paradise and heard words too sacred to tell, which a human is not permitted to utter (2 Cor. 12.2-4). Was the man Paul spoke of the High Priest of the new creation temple—*Yeshua* the Messiah? Was this a reminder of Adam on Eden's mountain paradise in the Presence of God?

Noah's ark can be viewed as the bridge between de-creation and re-creation designed to preserve life, protect against cosmic enemies, and house the Divine Presence. Building the ark can be pictured as a re-enactment of the creation of the universe. Return from exile was also a re-creation event.

Rebuilding the Temple signified the restoration of Israel's king to the throne. It meant that order and rest could now permeate the world.

Altar As Mountain

"The Temple was located on the highest peak on earth, very near heaven and facing its heavenly counterpart, the Sanctuary On High. The Temple symbolically represented the entire universe and each and every rite performed in it affected that part or aspect of nature of which the rite was reminiscent. The very existence of the entire world depended on it" (Patai 1967: 221). Mount Zion, home to Solomon's Temple, was seen as both the point of creation and the gateway to heaven. "His Holy mountain—a beautiful height—the joy of the whole earth. Mount Zion on the northern side of the city of the great King" (Ps. 48.3).

The Temple altar resembled Mount Zion in miniature—a replication of the cosmic mountain. Located at the intersection of Heaven and Earth, it was the transition point between the sacred and profane, the holy and the common. Rituals performed at the altar had an effect on the natural order of the universe with the purpose for the offerings being to restore creation and renew mankind's relationship with God. "Believing altars to have been the center of the covenant... the altar itself was a symbolic representation of cosmic mountain, the heavenly mountain of God, site of the Lord's cosmic throne" (2015: 90). The great altar in Jerusalem's Temple was given the name "Mountain of God" (Barker 2008: 32).

The altar, designed in three levels, was patterned after the cosmic mountain. The top called *har'el* or "Mountain of God" represented heaven (Ezek. 43.13-16). A large middle section represented the earth and was called the *soviv* or surround. This level included a protrusion that enabled the priests access to the horns of the altar in order to sprinkle the blood. A wide red line surrounded the middle level: blood splashed above the line dealt with sins against heaven, and blood splashed below the line dealt with sins against man and the earth. The blood acted as a disinfectant that would cleanse the altar from all impurities and by extension cleanse the cosmos. At the lowest level was the base or foundation called the bosom of the earth or the place where the "sea has been restrained"(14). According to Morales, this gives the altar a cosmic significance (2012: 251). Underneath the altar lay the great pit which represented the underworld or *she'ol*. Every seven years, Temple priests went underneath the altar to clean off the blood-caked residue. (A waterway constructed through the courtyard enabled them to flood the area and cleanse everything on the floor).

The fire offerings symbolized the sacramental presence of God. "The glory of *Adonai* settled upon Mount Sinai and the cloud covered it for six days. Then on the seventh day He called to Moses out of the midst of the cloud. "The appearance of the glory of *Adonai* was like a consuming fire on top of the mountain in the sight of the *Benei Yisrael* [children of Israel]" (Ex. 24.15-17). The seven days of creation are aligned with the forming of the mountain and with the altar which represented the presence of *YHWH* interpreted as a fiery essence (Morales 2012: 243). The fire offering ascending to *YHWH's* domain, via the smoke, invokes an image of the fiery presence of God on Sinai's summit. "The theophany transferred from the mountain to the altar" (Dozeman 2009: 564).

The priests' altar duties facilitated the crossing of boundaries, that is, moving from the realm of the profane or common to the sacred or holy. Burning the sacrifice was the exclusive right of priests whose service involved this transference of realms. Smoke from the burning animal rose up from the earthly plane to the heavenly realm and, ultimately, to the ownership of *YHWH*. The altar was the exclusive domain of the priests. Their role was to ascend the altar to serve as mediators between Heaven and Earth, between God and man, and to keep the cosmos cleansed by splashing the blood against the altar. Just as the mountain served as the bulwark against the forces of chaos, the altar too served as a place of divine, covenantal protection.

In the Second Temple, the smoke produced as the High Priest placed the incense on the shovelful of coals in the Holy of Holies on *Yom Kippur* (the Day of Atonement) was compared to a cloud. A parallel seems clear in that Moses ascended the mountain and entered into the cloud on Sinai's summit. The cloud, like the columns of smoke, ushered the priest into God's presence.

The altar, inhabited by the sanctifying presence of God, was a place of covenantal blessing and worship where "[d]eity and humanity [could] meet in communion on the cosmic mountain for a mutual act of worship and the renewal of creation" (Sailhammer 1992: 128). Worship that began at the foot of the mountain with the smoke rising from the altar would be consummated at the top of the mountain in His presence.

Sailhammer also notes that the building of an altar always followed a major act of God's salvation, such as God rescuing Noah from the flood or God delivering Moses and the Children of Israel from the grip of Pharaoh (128-9). Noah offering up a sacrifice on the altar after the ark came to rest on Ararat seems to portray worship as the first act of the new creation. Noah built an altar where the seas had been just as the first fixed point of creation, the cosmic mountain, formed out of the seas. Sailhammer further suggests, "[p]erhaps the manner of worship experienced in Exodus (24) reflects a pattern inherent in the divine ordering of creation. It reveals the framework of God's design for the ideal universe... worship linked with the creation of a new community after the pattern of the creation of the cosmos" (129).

CHAPTER THREE

HISTORY

Yeshua answered, My kingship is not of this world;
if my kingship were of this world, my servants
would fight, that I might not be handed over to
the Jews; but my kingship is not from the world.
John 18.36 RSV

A Little Bit of History

Around 6000 BCE, irrigation was first developed in the foot-hills of the Zagros mountains (SE Turkey). As farmers settled the region, a burgeoning agricultural trade spread through-out the Fertile Crescent into southern Mesopotamia. Smaller villages grew into large urban centers called city-states. Sumer, located in the southern regions of the Tigris and Euphrates rivers, soon emerged as the world's first civilization (c. 4000 BCE). At first, the low-lying plains were problematic for food production due to the arid landscape. With the advancement of irrigation technology, grain production soon increased dramatically, and grain became the life-blood for the region's growing population. Wheat's capacity for long-term storage led to an explosion in trade throughout Mesopotamia. Overall, Sumer had very few natural resources—little mineral wealth, or wood for building, and a shortage of stone.

Urbanization peaked in the early third millennium BCE, and Uruk, Sumer's most important and influential city, reached nearly 50,000 residents. Its Aramaic name, Erech, is found in the Bible (Gen. 10.10). Uruk's close proximity to the Euphrates river meant an abundance of silt deposits left behind from annual flooding, which made for highly productive farmland along the river banks. Eventually, a network of dikes and canals harnessed the flood waters for those towns and villages located further inland.

The urban revolution eventually transformed the Fertile Crescent into a highly civilized, complex society controlled by a king and his family who owned most of the real estate. The city-state's agricultural industry fell under the auspices of its political elites who needed slave labor for large-scale infrastructure projects. Political power rested with those who managed food production, storage, and distribution. In addition, a new class of professional craftsmen emerged who were skilled in the manufacturing of other goods for trade. City administrators developed a system of symbols to record these economic transactions. In the Early Dynastic period (2900-2350 BCE), a wedge-shaped stylus was invented for inscribing economic information on clay tablets. After the region's great flood, writing officially emerged under the rulership of King Enmerkar of Uruk.

Kingship in ancient Sumer was a divine institution that descended from heaven. The Sumerian King List records eight rulers in the pre-flood era who reigned for fantastically long periods of time, some spanning over tens of thousands of years. Despite suggestions that the list was fictional, it still served as a powerful symbol for the dynasty's legitimacy. Some scholars believe this antediluvian king list was a work of political propaganda specifically designed to help the rulers of the Isin dynasty take over the region. At least eighteen different king lists have been uncovered (with no two the same), although it is believed they derived from a single account. The most extensive version is the Weld-Blundell Prism found in the Ashmolean Museum's cuneiform collection in Oxford, England. It remains the most complete list and provides a chronological framework for kingship in Sumeria.

Scholars suggest the first flood story was written down in Sumer, modified during the early Babylonian period, and later revised by the Assyrians. Each dynastic period focused on a particular flood hero: Ziusudra in the Sumerian period, Atrahasis in the Akkadian, and Utnapistim, from the *Epic of Gilgamesh*, in the early Babylonian/Mesopotamian period. The Hebrew scribes likely transformed Israel's own flood story during the post-exilic period to showcase their hero-king, Noah, whom *YHWH* had commanded to build an ark to save His people. The story's purpose was to bring a message of hope and salvation to Israel during their exilic experience.

Copies of the *Epic of Gilgamesh* were first discovered in 1849 CE on clay tablets located in the library of the Assyrian king, Assurbanipal (668–627 BCE) in Nineveh. This twelve-tablet Akkadian version of the epic is the best known. Assyriologist George Smith, when translating the Babylonian account of the flood, discovered a ship that rested on the mountains of Nizir—a detail eerily similar to the ark landing on Mt. Ararat in the Genesis story. Smith recounted this discovery in his book, *The Chaldean Account of Genesis (1872)*.

In the Babylonian period, the *Epic of Gilgamesh*'s flood hero was Utnapishtim. The epic tells his story in Tablet XI: Utnapishtim builds a boat and saves his family along with the animals by outwitting the gods. Gilgamesh, the warrior-king who ruled Uruk in the third millennium (2900-2500 BCE), sought out Utnapishtim to discover the key to immortality, which kings in the ancient world desired above all else. Gilgamesh's adventures were strung together and rewritten many times over the centuries. Later Mesopotamian kings invoked his name in order to associate his lineage with their own.

Uruk, considered the first true city of the region, boasted a host of architectural advances. A stair-stepped, stone structure located in the heart of the city featured a temple for the patron god Inanna—Uruk's true owner. Called the Great White Temple, it served as the city's administrative center from which the king, appointed by Inanna, ruled. In this early phase of civilization, cities housed only public buildings; the surrounding environs were where the commoners resided. The earliest form of government was the "general assembly" (c. 2900 BCE) which lasted only a brief time when the cosmos was viewed as a state in itself and the institution of kingship was born. Centralized authority became the new political order. The city was now the center for all economic, political, and cultural activity. An "assembly of the gods" is featured in the book of Psalms (82.1) where God sits to judge the gods' claims of a right to divinity.

Conflict soon arose between the various city-states when foreign invaders threatened stability. By the mid-third millennium, secular rulers usurped political and economic control as they vied for strategic advantage. Power struggles ensued over the region's resources: land, waterways, and trade routes. History's first world conqueror, Sargon I of Akkad, arrived on the scene after the flood and seized the Sumerian city of Kish in 2334 BCE. From there, he conquered vast amounts of territory to become chief overlord of Sumer and Akkad.

Rulers used military might, technology, and economic dominance to crush opposition and centralize control away from the city-state. The story of the Tower of Babel illustrates how these "empire builders" operated. Brick technology (c. 3100 BCE) opened the door to slavery, as human labor was needed to complete the kings' building projects. Since the new burnt-brick technology was expensive, it was used only for the most important buildings located in the cities: palaces, temples, granaries, and ziggurats. Bitumen technology developed simultaneously and was used for mortar to strengthen the walls of the public sector buildings, making them stronger than either rock or iron. With the latest technology in the hands of the ruling elites, human exploitation followed. Though this technology was beneficial for everyone, it was also a stepping stone for the political class to gain more power at the expense of the common people.

Brick and bitumen technology appears in the Tower of Babel story. The text seems to indicate *YHWH's* indictment of the people for building the city, and especially the tower, in an effort to reach heaven. Dr. John Walton thinks the story is actually emphasizing historical patterns of migration, the establishing of permanent settlements, and the development of urbanization. Could this be? Is Genesis (11) in fact showcasing the consequences of urbanization and not the people's disobedience in building the city and tower?

Scattering was the logical answer for the problems of overpopulation, urbanization, competition for limited grazing land, and lack of water resources. The story of Abraham and Lot comes to mind; they separated because the land could not support all of their flocks and tents. Lot headed east to the cities of the well-watered plains of the Jordan (east signifying a move away from the presence of God and towards evil); Abraham chose to remain in Canaan and to settle in the mountains near Hebron.

Migration from Northern Mesopotamia first began during the Ubaid period (5000-3500 BCE). In Genesis (11), people were migrating east (possibly the descendants of Shem) to the Plains of Shinar. According to historians, as water levels dropped in the Persian Gulf and the Tigris and Euphrates rivers began to recede, settlements sprung up all over the southern region. Previously, regular flooding from the rivers had covered large tracts of land making permanent settlement impossible (Walton 2006: 119-121).

Were the builders of the tower attempting to prevent a "scattering" by pursuing urbanization (Walton, 1995)? Did *YHWH* scatter the people in response to centralized control, which was inevitable when cities began to urbanize? The ancients saw cities as dark places where evil resided. Were *YHWH's* actions designed to interrupt their urbanization process in order to protect His people? If so, then scattering should be seen as an act of mercy and compassion because it was the antidote to concentrated power.

✡   ✡   ✡

The following fictional account imagines the historical and mythological world of Sumer and its kings before the flood and its relationship to various characters in the Bible. So far, no inscriptions verify the names of the antediluvian (pre-flood) kings. Dating is also problematic as scholars and archaeologists simply do not have any link to datable historic events. Most agree the first King of Sumer was Alulim. Most also agree the eighth and final king was Ubara-tutu whose reign ended with a cataclysmic flood that swept away the known world. Excavations of Ur by Leonard Wooley revealed an eight-foot layer of silt and clay consistent with sediment from the Euphrates. Some say this supports a catastrophic flood around 2900-2800 BCE.

Adam was buried at the entrance to *Gan Eden*, the Garden in Eden, at *Macpelah*, appropriately named the "cave of the companions," for *Chavah*, mother of the living, would soon join him in Paradise. Family and friends gathered to share stories in which they fondly remembered *Adam Ben Elohim*, the Son of God. Adam's exile from the Garden meant the forfeiture of God's design of peace on earth and good will of men towards one another. The corrupt nature of mankind would continually rear its ugly head, first through families and clans and then through tyrannical kings and nations—all in the pursuit of power. Going back to the actions of the serpent king in the garden, the strategy was lies, propaganda, and corruption. Wicked rulers would oppress, enslave, and even murder masses of humanity until the King of Kings finally said, "Enough!"

On this day, Adam's mourners chose not to lament his failure to fulfill their clan's destiny—though the fullness of his regnal years, which should have been one thousand, had been cut short by seventy due to his rebellion against the One True God. Gathering at the entrance to the mountain tomb complex, the large crowd lifted their voices and sang blessings in angelic tones to celebrate the resurrection of the dead: "You are eternally mighty my Lord, the Resuscitator of the dead, abundantly able to save… You O King who causes death and restores life and makes salvation sprout. And you are faithful to resuscitate the dead." Adam, Son of God, the first of the covenant kings, was laid to rest in the burial cave of the patriarchs and their wives. His body, sown in corruption, would soon be raised incorruptible to become a life-giving being, dwelling forever in the presence of His God.

The clan sat *shiva*, mourning the required seven days. Those in the immediate family sat on hard, wooden benches positioned lower than their visitors. The family received words of condolence and comfort from the members of the clan. They remembered how *YHWH* had ultimately delivered Adam from the clutches of tyranny. Though he lost his Garden inheritance, Adam was remembered as a man who served God in the midst of much suffering and through endless trials and tribulations. He had learned over time how to be fruitful and how to fill the earth. He had learned how to overcome thorns and thistles and nutrient-depleted soil. Adam had also faithfully maintained his marriage vows to his precious wife, *Chavah*, unlike those in the line of his son Cain.

Chanting in low tones, the family recited the Mourner's Kaddish: "May His great Name grow exalted and sanctified... May He give reign to His Kingship and cause his salvation to sprout and bring near His Messiah." They would patiently await God's promise of a future king, the Messiah, a Son of God who would fulfill the one thousand regnal years.

Seth was next in line. He had helped to restore order to his family after the chaos of losing two sons. He was the heir in whom Adam put his trust to carry on the family traditions. Seth, meaning the seed who *YHWH* provided, would keep the dynasty alive. Adam had mentored him in livestock breeding and managing the flocks. From a young age, Seth had learned the proper protocols for the ritual slaughter of the animals and for offering up the sacred meat to *YHWH*. Seth excelled in both animal husbandry and crop production, as well as irrigation techniques. Working with Adam had created a close bond between the two; Adam's death came as a severe blow.

Chavah put on a brave face for the family. She encouraged the little ones lest they fall into despair. But as she sat alone at night in front of the fire pit, mesmerized by the burning embers, she cried both tears of joy and sadness as she reflected on the pivotal moments of her life with Adam. She remembered affectionately the day Cain was born, though those thoughts were bittersweet. He had been the purest expression of the love Adam and *Chavah* shared for one another. She held out hope for him still; after all, he was *kanah*: his mother's prized possession. She recalled thinking, "I have possessed a man by the help of *YHWH*." From the time her second son, Abel, was born, she was haunted by a sense of foreboding that somehow life would flow out from him early on, but she never imagined it would be in such a violent manner. She couldn't have known she would lose both sons at the same time: one to death, the other to exile.

Before tragedy struck, Adam had divided the leadership of the clan between Cain and Abel. Cain worked the fields to provide food for the family and first fruits to his God. His priestly service was fulfilled through a special kinship with the adamah: the earth. Cain inherited his father's special skill for gardening—a vocation he never fully embraced. Though he brought the offerings from the earth to *YHWH*, he always felt the work was beneath him. Hunting was more his desire, and he felt he should have had a larger role in raising livestock and hunting game. *Chavah* never stopped wondering if she could have done more to encourage him in his role.

Abel shepherded the flocks for the family. Daily, he brought the burnt offering to *YHWH* on behalf of the clan. Abel, the shepherd king, was the apple of his father's eye. Cain, the gardener king, was *Chavah's* special firstborn. A bitter rivalry arose between the herdsman and the farmer; the firstborn continually felt displaced by the second born.

Every morning, Cain ground the semolina and mixed it with water and salt. He took a tenth of an *ephah* of whole flour, divided it in two, and prepared one part for the morning offering and the other for the afternoon. He mixed three logs of oil into the fine flour then ascended the altar with one portion, along with a handful of frankincense, and placed the offering on the fire. Cain watched as it was totally consumed. The *minchah*, or grain offering, acknowledged Cain's dedication to God and his thankfulness for God's provision. On one particular morning, a morning *Chavah* would never forget, Cain raced to the altar with his grain offering ahead of Abel whose burnt offering was to be offered first.

The burnt offering was a sign of submission to the Master of the Universe. Burning the whole animal apart from its skin symbolized a life of total consecration to God. Twice daily, the burnt and grain offerings were consumed by fire. A thick, billowy column of smoke rose like a cloud as *YHWH* breathed in the sweet aroma of the meat and then the grain.

These acts connected Heaven and Earth in the place where *YHWH* chose to put His name. On this day, however, *YHWH* rejected Cain's offering. In anger, Cain killed his brother Abel at the altar.

As punishment, Cain was exiled from the clan to face life in the wilderness—a harsh, barren, lifeless environment without water and filled with dangerous wild beasts. He tried to work the ground using his expert skills, but the land never produced; his relationship with the earth was forever broken. Though *Chavah* never stopped hoping that her firstborn would miraculously return, Cain's exile led him eastward—away from the safety of the clan and away from the Presence of the One True God. The land to the east was known as Nod. It was a place of permanent separation filled with all manner of evil.

Cain's tribal identity was now lost, along with *YHWH's* covenant protection, but *YHWH* promised to place a mark on Cain to safeguard him from evil men. This mark, pressed deeply into his skin, would show all those who met him to whom he belonged. For Cain, the mark was a constant reminder that though he once was a part of the royal household of Adam, he had rejected that status. Cain took some comfort in the fact that if he were killed his murderer would receive vengeance sevenfold. He resigned himself to never returning home to his father's house by the Great Sea.

Cain wandered the Fertile Crescent as a marked man reduced to hunting wild beasts. For the ancients, wild beasts were the untamed forces that created chaos. Faced with recurring threats from roving bands of marauders and harsh terrain, Cain joined a caravansary headed to the land of Sumer—the land of the black-headed people. The name Sumer was first given by shepherd/kings who created a form of government called *ki-en-gi*: *ki* for land, *en* for lord or priest, and *gi* for civilized.

Cain's journey ended at the city of Uruk located on the banks of the Euphrates River. He settled in and began plotting his rise to chief Abgal—a common epithet for the ruling class. He went to work building the small agricultural settlement into an economic powerhouse. With great cunning and superb hunting skills, he set Uruk on a course of urbanization. In order to fully accomplish his plan, though, he would need to be appointed ruler of Uruk by the goddess Inanna.

One day in a vision, Cain saw a jewel-bedecked figure who descended from heaven wearing a crown. Cain knew rulership in Sumer was manifested in the stars, especially through the most prominent constellation of all: Orion (also called Nephila, whose descendants were called the *Nephilim*). Orion was indeed *the* most dazzling of all the constellations. Cain pictured himself within its stars carrying a club upraised in his right hand. To Cain, the seven stars of Orion were *the* sign he would become king. After all, Orion was chief among the hunter-warriors that Mesopotamian kings adopted for their emblem. Confident, he pondered his next move.

Uruk was the first city to be centered around a temple to the local god. It featured a stepped tower called the Anu Ziggurat on which the White Temple for the goddess Inanna was built. Towering above the city, the temple signified Inanna's ever-increasing political authority. A stone statue of finely chiseled, white marble stood proudly displaying her image of renewal and fertility. In reality, Inanna was cold and calculating—qualities she happily instilled in her worshippers as they celebrated her cultic rituals. The ziggurat itself was a source of architectural pride for the gods, that is, until a great flood buried it in the silt and debris of the Euphrates river.

At first, the city was governed by a general assembly of citizens under Inanna's jurisdiction. She eventually replaced them with a king who ruled and reigned on her behalf. The opinions of the assembly's older members still carried some weight. Most of their decisions, though tempered by communal wisdom, were vetoed by the king. The assembly did exercise some clout when a crisis loomed large over the community and devastating floods brought on by the gods remained a major source of concern every spring.

Uruk's explosive growth coincided with Cain's meteoric rise to power. The prosperity experienced by the city provided the upper classes the opportunity to indulge in leisurely pursuits and creature comforts. Once a man who knew only deprivation, Cain now fully embraced the ease and economic advantages of city life. His only obstacle to obtaining full control would come from another king in the region, Alulim, whose rulership was deemed magnificent by his citizens. Alulim was the first of the Apkallu kings who attained the status of demi-god in Eridu of Sumer. The Apkallu themselves were a special breed of fish-like men created from the apsu: the primeval sea connected to the underworld.

Twenty-five kilometers north of Uruk, on the banks of the Tigris, King Alulim built a summer palace in the city of Shuruppak. He assembled a team of highly experienced artisans and craftsmen to construct a sprawling ziggurat complex dedicated to Ninlil: the goddess of grain and air. Shuruppak would be ground zero for the coming calamity caused by a catastrophic flood. Though no one suspected a flood at the time, the goddess Ninlil secretly instructed Ziusudra to build a boat in Shuruppak to ride out the disaster with his family.

Alulim, whose name was associated with a glittering ram, claimed his kingship was from Heaven. At first he swore allegiance to Anu, the supreme god of Heaven and Earth, but Anu would eventually be replaced by his granddaughter Inanna. Alulim of Eridu, recognized as Sumer's first demi-god, was also the first to embody the constellation Orion known as the giant in the sky. Cain planned to usurp his role.

One day while fishing in the Persian Gulf, a South Wind came up quickly and capsized Alulim's boat. He nearly drowned. In retaliation, King Alulim broke the wing of the South Wind which prevented it from blowing for a full seven days. The sky god Anu was enraged, and he demanded

Alulim appear immediately before his heavenly court. Before appearing, Alulim sought divine counsel from Eridu's patron god Ea. Ea feared Anu would offer betrayed Alulim the food of eternal life which would allow him to usurp Anu's own standing in Eridu. Considering this year, he chose to betray Alulim. Ea convinced Alulim to reject Anu's offer. Anu did offer Alulim the food and was perplexed by Alulim's rejection. In anger, he sent him away. Alulim, forced to retreat to his summer palace in Shuruppak, now understood his days were numbered and eternal life was no longer within reach. He also knew this incident would give his enemy Cain a strategic advantage.

Inanna remained Mesopotamia's most popular goddess. She once stole the Meh (the Sumerian tablets for divine decrees that governed the universe) from her father Enki who ruled the sacred city of Eridu before Ea. Taking the Meh resulted in the transfer of power from Eridu to Uruk. Alulim desperately wanted them back in order to fulfill his destiny, and he was willing to go to war with Inanna to reclaim Eridu's rightful place.

Enki retaliated against Inanna for stealing the Meh. He bribed her king and chief gardener to purposely neglect the plants and shrubs inside the White Temple complex. Though her precious hupulu, a large poplar tree known for its giant canopy, was spared, Inanna was enraged over this act of betrayal. She cursed the lands around Sumer and plotted her revenge. She would wait patiently, however, before enacting her plan; at just the right time, she would send a deluge that would wipe out everything in the region. Nothing would stand in her way.

Cain presented his case to Inanna: his gardening skills qualified him to rule Uruk, and his hunting skills would aid in tracking down her former chief gardener. Cain boasted of his knowledge of agricultural technology and spoke glowingly of his father's skill in horticulture which was legendary throughout the known world. Rumors still swirled, however, that giant *Cheruvim* waving fiery swords had cut off access to the great Garden in Eden by the Sea. Cain revealed the family secret that his father and mother had lost their way to the Tree of Life and with it all hope of immortality. He was convinced immortality would be within *his* reach, however, should he receive the appointment.

Cain soon reaped the rewards bestowed upon the aristocratic class. With his position as king and chief gardener secured, he began manipulating the economic records. He siphoned profits from local artisans and craftsmen and extorted those in positions of power who might stand in his way. Hush money was regularly used to pay local officials for their silence. He built a secret police force to protect against possible uprisings. Cain gathered personal information on all Uruk's citizens—always looking for weakness, compromise, or any illegality that could force them to work on his behalf. He used fear and intimidation tactics to successfully remove the opposition.

Cain's brutality against those who resisted authority became legendary throughout Sumer. Most simply acquiesced to protect themselves and their families from prison, torture, or worse. Propaganda and lies were the weapons of his warfare, and he took full advantage of his newly won warrior-king status in order to abuse the people. His excessive use of force led to a populace who cowered in fear. He demanded total allegiance and destroyed any who stood in his way.

Cain sent spies to Eridu to work undercover in King Alulim's household. They gathered intelligence on the entire family (including the king's financial transactions), the very latest in technological advances, and the movements of palace courtiers and guards. From Uruk, Cain soon expanded his rule to Eridu and finally into Alulim's court. Alulim's daughter, Ashan, who served as priestess at the Abzu temple of the god Enki, secretly pursued a relationship with Cain.

She bore a son and Cain named him *Enoch*. Having successfully infiltrated Alulim's city-state through marriage and palace intrigue, Cain easily forced the king from his throne.

Following Alulim, a succession of Sumerian kings rose up who ruled for extended periods of time and who continually sought revenge against the line of Cain. For his part, Cain passed on his penchant for evil to his progeny Lamech who also murdered a man. Lamech then took captive the man's wife and her sister adding them to his harem. Prior to the great flood, Cain was killed by Lamech who mistook him for a wild beast trying to attack inside the palace courtyard. Confused by the dark shadows jostling in the South Wind, he picked up a giant stone and smashed it over Cain's head. The untamed forces that created chaos were about to be unleashed.

By the tenth generation from Adam, Sumeria's powerful kings had plunged the entire world into chaos through all manner of violence and corruption. There was little regard for the needs and concerns of humanity. Violence became the solution for solving conflict. The coming great flood would be the final blow to the region and would ultimately lead to mass starvation and death. The gods were delighted; the flood would finally solve the problem of overpopulation. Inanna's reputation for cold, calculating evil would now be realized.

The annual flooding of the Tigris and Euphrates was often very destructive. Such was the case one particularly wet spring during the reign of the eighth antediluvian King of Sumer, Ubara-tutu of Shuruppak. He was said to have entered heaven without dying, but in reality he disappeared when a catastrophic flood swept over the known world.

Sons of God And The Daughters of Men

When humankind began to multiply on the face of the ground and daughters were born to them, then the sons of God saw that the daughters of men were good and they took for themselves wives, any they chose. The *Nephilim* were on the earth in those days, and also afterward, whenever the sons of God came to the daughters of men, and gave birth to them. Those were the mighty men of old, men of renown.

GENESIS 6.1-2,4

Perhaps the most hotly debated and confusing passages in Scripture are the ones leading up to the flood. Meredith Kline in his article *"Divine Kingship and Genesis 6:1-4"* describes these verses as "raw mythology" that should be interpreted from the perspective of divine kingship. According to Kline, it was during the antediluvian period (before the flood) that kings, who were regarded as divine, took the title "son of god"—a title that was political in nature and related to royal authority. This title was a useful propaganda tool that advanced a king's political position over his rivals. Mythologically speaking, the pre-flood kings were regarded as divine beings born of the gods and further identified as heroes of old. Though mortal at birth, they became immortal at their enthronement.

The sons of god or *benei elohim* were considered royalty. These were not only the kings of city-states but were also members of the ruling class that included princes, noblemen, and the aristocracy. Born into the world of the elites, these "mighty men of renown" considered might and power their divine right. "Through them, the earth was filled with gifted rulers who exercised their stewardship of talent and dominion in the perfecting of the consecration of all sub-human creation to the interests of man as the royal representative and priest of God" (Kline 1962: 200). The Bible declares, "You are gods and you are all sons of *Elyon* yet you will die like men, and fall like any of the princes" (Ps. 82.6-7).

ANE scholars have put forth a number of interpretations for the meaning of "the sons of god," including angels, ANE kings who were divine, and/or some kind of otherworldly being. Some have also suggested a theory in which the sons of god were godly men from the line of Seth. In this theory, the daughters of men were ungodly descendants of Cain. Kline disagrees, however, explaining "the sons of god" in this case is a designation specifically pointing to the line of Cain. Though modern interpreters often identify the sons of god in a more spiritual sense, that is, godly men who are in covenant with *YHWH*. Kline posits that the idea of "man" as a "spiritual" son of god was unknown in the period before the Biblical flood (191).

The sons of god married the daughters of men, and their union produced great wickedness on the earth. "The *Nephilim* [translated giants or fallen ones] were also on the earth along with the daughters of men who gave birth to the *Gibborim* or mighty men of renown" (Gen. 6.4). According to Kline, the sons of god married their inferiors: the daughters of men. Together, they produced the *Nephilim* who spawned all manner of violence and corruption during the period before the flood (A popular view suggests the *Nephilim* were either divine or demonic beings who entered into marriage with the daughters of men to produce a race of non-terrestrial, giant-like beings).

During the pre-flood era, kings ruled large urban centers known as the city-state. The city-state was the foundation for the emergence of kingship which functioned under the sovereignty of a city's patron god (Gen. 4.16-24). "Kingship was of heavenly origin and, significantly, it numbered a god among its representatives" (Kline 1962: 199). Kline connects the sons of god, the *benei elohim*, with the dynasty of sacral kings reaching back before the flood to the Cainite lineage. Kline adds that the Cainite rulers esteemed themselves powerful in name and renown like the *Gibborim*.

Lamech, of the line of Cain, was the first to practice bigamy which eventually gave rise to the political institution known as the harem (Gen. 4.19). Kline suggests the account of Lamech is similar to the account of the *benei elohim* (Gen. 6) in which both take wives and bear children in order to advance their dynastic exploits. Rulers gained power by forging political alliances through marriage, specifically through the harem. Political alliances cemented a king's standing as he expanded his empire in honor of his patron god. These political partnerships thwarted most enemy opposition and maintained the king's power through the regnal inheritance of the royal seed.

In the ancient world, the harem was a political institution under the auspices of the king's court. The harem included rulers' wives, princesses, concubines, daughters of foreign nobility, and female servants of a conquered king. These women were lodged in the private quarters of the palace called the House of Women (Parpola 2012: 613-614). Young girls were trained for palace life in order to be given as gifts to kings or the aristocracy. Rules governing the harem were determined by royal edict; the harem provided the necessary education for the women to become wives of the ruling class.

A large number of these girls and women were even trained as court musicians. Royal courts generally featured a music director who was a government minister and one of the king's most trusted aides. Lamech's first wife, *Adah*, for example, gave birth to Jubal who was the "pioneer of all who skillfully handled stringed instruments and wind instruments" (Gen. 4.21). Could it be that the appellation "daughters of men" was a description for those of the king's harem who were raised up to marry royalty? Is it possible marriage between the aristocracy and the women of the harem was being compared to the "divine" sons of god marrying the daughters of "mortal" men? (In the pre-flood era, a divine king was viewed as immortal.) It is worth noting that the daughters of men were described as "good" meaning they had a specific function and purpose, that is, to be fruit producers for the empire by bringing forth heirs.

According to Kline, Cainite kingship eventually produced a state of tyranny and corruption intolerable to the God of

Heaven (Kline 1962: 195). "By reason of the polygamy and tyranny practiced by the dynasty of the *benei elohim*, sons of god in the name of the divine-royal prerogative and justice, the earth became corrupt before God and filled with violence and so hasted to destruction" (196). Kline suggests that failure in matters of royal enterprise was due to Cain's lineage violating God's marriage decree which in turn produced chaos. This resulted in civilization's downward spiral of immorality, violence, and corruption.

YHWH's creational blueprint signified a state of order regarding marriage, the family, and godly labor. The Bible's creation story subverted the ways of world empire when it championed, "a man will leave his father and mother and cling to his wife and the two will become one flesh" (Gen. 2.24). The flood ultimately caused the regnal aspirations of the Cainite line to perish in the waters of God's divine judgment. At the same time, Adam's royal seed Noah preserved kingship, marriage, and the blessings of agricultural service.

The Creator God, *YHWH*, bestowed upon Adam rulership of the earth. Adam's divine mandate was to subdue and to cultivate—a mission carried out through marriage and agricultural labor. After the flood, this royal mandate was re-instituted through Noah who preserved the institution of marriage by saving his wife and his sons and their wives (as well as their future seed), and by cultivating a vineyard. "For within the ark there was found the paradisiacal kingdom of God renewed in miniature with regal Noah, scion of Seth's faithful dynasty, together with his princely heirs established in dominion over the representatives of all the sub-human creation and triumphant over the natural elements" (Kline 1962: 200). And so Noah, royal servant and Son of God, in covenant with *YHWH*, emerged from the ark as the "new born" king raised up to rule over a cleansed and renewed earth. His enthronement, considered a re-creation event, functioned not only as a subversive response to the political powers of the day but also as a de-construction of the competing flood stories belonging to those same powers.

Kingship, first established in Sumer, was lowered from heaven. The Sumerian King List records the first eight kings who ruled over five cities in ancient Mesopotamia for excessively long periods. For example, in Eridu, Alulim became king and reigned 28,000 years; Dumuzi, a shepherd (ruler), ruled 36,000 years. In total, these eight kings ruled 241,000 years, and then the flood swept over the earth. John Walton believes the exaggerated reigns could be related to the extended lifespans of the early Biblical patriarchs (by dropping Adam and Noah from the list there are eight patriarchs).

Is it possible the patriarchs' long lifespans (Gen. 5) were tied to kingship and regnal years? Walton suggests the reigns of the pre-flood kings and the lifespans of the patriarchs are numerically equivalent if the number base is changed from sexagesimal (a base 60 numbering system) to the decimal system. In addition, the Sumerian king list did not represent a straight line succession but rather overlapping dynasties, just as with the patriarch's lifespans. The regnal years of Israel and Judah's kings also overlap making an accurate counting of their reigns difficult. (See *The Mysterious Numbers of the Hebrew Kings* by Edwin Thiele for an analysis of Israel's over-lapping regnal years).

Additionally, in Genesis (6) God declares, "My Spirit will not remain with humankind forever, since they are flesh. So their days will be 120 years." Most have taken this to mean that the lifespan of humanity would be reduced to 120 years after the flood while some think this is referring to the number of years it took Noah to build the ark. However, if the extended lifespans of the patriarchs (Genesis 5) in the pre-flood era are related to kingship, this could suggest a shortening of regnal years. Why 120? Is it connected to the sexagesimal numbering system of the ancient world? Is there a hidden message related to the exiles returning from Babylon that confirmed Israel's united monarchy would be restored based on the collective 120-year reign of Saul, David, and Solomon? Is 120 also related to Moses who, as God's chosen ruler over Israel, ultimately delivered them from the slavery of Egypt's pharaoh? Moses lived to 120 years. Was 120 meant to be understood as a regnal expression? Walton reminds us that our Biblical focus should be on what kingship communicated to the world (Longman III & Walton 2018: 20).

After the flood, kingship was again lowered from heaven. The Bible declares Nimrod a mighty hunter, a *Gibborim* in the land (Gen. 10.8-10), who made a great name for himself. Nimrod, of the line of Ham, ruled over the great cities of the Land of Shinar: Babel, Erech, Akkad, and Calneh. The cultural and political milieu of the pre-flood era returned, and the *Gibborim* continued using the same tactics in exercising political power. They enslaved their subjects, took control of the region, and again resorted to violence in the pursuit of power. These rulers rejected *YHWH's* sovereignty, until at the Tower of Babel, the world was again ripe for judgment.

Kingship is a central theme in the Bible, and the Bible often presents the failures of human kings. We might ask how the Kingdom of God can manifest itself on the earth through human agency in building a foundation of righteousness and justice for its people. Deuteronomy instructs that the king was not to be like the *Gibborim* who filled the earth with violence and corruption. The king was not to commit injustice against the weak and the powerless. The king was to judge rightly while breaking the back of those who oppressed his people (Kline 1962: 203). The king was not to multiply wives unto himself, nor horses, nor silver and gold (Deut. 17.14-17). For Israel and the world, kingship would reach its pinnacle only under the sovereignty of *YHWH* who sent His heir, *Yeshua* the Messiah, Son of God, to remove chaos, restore order, and renew the cosmos.

Kingship And The Harem

According to many scholars, the Bible was formulated during Israel's post-exilic period. That said, it's likely the Genesis flood story was retold with that view in mind. The exiles were desperate to make sense of their situation. They asked why *YHWH* allowed their sacred Temple to be destroyed by the Babylonians, why the monarchy was upended, and why they were sent into exile as punishment. Retelling the flood story in order to deconstruct the nations' flood myths gave them the assurance *YHWH* would triumph: rebuild His Holy Temple, rescue the exiles, and restore the *Davidic* dynasty.

The fall of Jerusalem (586-7 BCE) and the destruction of the Temple left the nation and the monarchy in shambles; it looked to be the "end" of David's everlasting kingdom. In the eyes of the world, Israel had been shamed and humiliated. After seventy years in Babylon, some exiles returned to the land with a renewed sense of hope that the *Davidic* branch (Zech. 3.8) would soon sprout again (2 Samuel 7). A possible foreshadowing of the restoration appeared in the flood story when a dove returned to the ark with a torn olive leaf in its beak. King David once declared, "[I] am like an olive tree flourishing in the House of God" (Ps. 52.10a). Was the olive leaf the sign of the renewal of the kingdom after exile?

David compared his royal dynasty to an olive tree for its longevity (they can live for thousands of years) and for its ability to regenerate itself from the roots even if its branches and trunk are destroyed. Trees in the ANE represented kings; trees sprouting indicated the perpetuation of the dynasty. They symbolized divinity and were regarded as oracles, vehicles of knowledge and wisdom, through which the divine communicated (George and George 2014: 144).

Jeremiah (11.16-17) refers to the leaders of the House of Israel as a once thriving olive tree that the Lord destroyed by setting it on fire and breaking its branches. Jeremiah was holding the leadership responsible for the coming destruction by the Babylonians because they had failed to obey the covenant. Paul speaks of the restoration of the whole House of Israel, the dynasty of King David, when the natural branches are grafted into the trunk of the cultivated olive tree (Romans 11).

Peter Enns explains that after the exile Israel never again recreated the eternal dynasty as it was during the reigns of David and Solomon. Those who returned remained a subjugated people under Greece, Rome, and even the Hasmonean empire. Hope of restoring the monarchy ended in 70 CE with the Jewish Revolt when Rome finally crushed all resistance. Scattered throughout the Roman empire, the Jewish people would have to function outside the land, without a temple and king and without a national identity. "Judaism and the early Jesus movement transformed the nationalistic tradition of old to address the non-nationalistic reality of post 70 CE world" (Enns 2012: 1-11).

David ushered in a monarchical golden age after defeating Israel's enemies who had created chaos for the nation. He then provided the blueprint for his son Solomon to build a glorious Temple for *YHWH's* Presence and to preserve the *Davidic* dynasty. Noah, in rescuing his family from the waters of chaos, confirmed the continuation of the line of Adam. In building the ark/temple, Noah established a place where God's sovereign rule would remain. King David's military victories were a type of rebirth for the nation likened to God's primeval victory over the waters of chaos.

Throughout his reign, King David established important political and commercial alliances with neighboring states. This period was marked by political autonomy for the Jewish people as well as financial prosperity. David's son Solomon (970-931 BCE is the general consensus) was also a savvy political player, expanding the empire at a time when Egypt was weak and Mesopotamia was no threat. Solomon imported and exported military equipment, traded for chariots and horses with the Hittites and others, and became the world's foremost international arms dealer. War was big business. "Now the weight of gold that came to Solomon was 666 talents besides what was from the merchants from the traffic of traders, and from all the kings of Arabia and the governors of the region" (I Kings 10.14-15). An inevitable consequence of buying and selling weapons of war, Solomon sometimes supplied his enemies with the armaments used against Israel.

Solomon engaged in maritime commerce with the Phoenicians, trading gold and tropical products. He expanded trade routes into Africa, Asia Minor, and Arabia, and he built a fleet of ships in *Ezion-Geber* staffed with sailors who seized 420 talents of gold from Ophir (1 Kings 9.26-28). The chariot city of Megiddo was established as a strategic administrative and military center. Located on the international highway between Egypt and Damascus on a hill overlooking the Jezreel valley, Megiddo reached its zenith under King Solomon in the tenth century BCE. Over the next few centuries, numerous battles were fought for control of the city and nearby trade routes. Megiddo was finally settled at the end of the sixth millennium BCE with the Assyrians establishing a seat of government during the reign of Jeroboam II, King of Israel. King Josiah of Judah, an ally of the Neo-Babylonians, was slain on the plains of Megiddo by Pharaoh Necho of Egypt.

Solomon inserted his most trusted friends in key positions and centralized his authority by organizing the nation into districts instead of tribes (I Kings 4.7-19). He built up his capital city, Jerusalem. He constructed the Holy Temple, and he built a magnificent palace that included a large harem. Major fortifications were also erected for chariot cities using local and foreign slave labor. Solomon enacted a variety of reforms that included financial windfall through taxation, compulsory military service, and tribute from foreign countries. He often used his great wealth to expand the kingdom at the expense of the poor and the needy. In time, Solomon became as Egypt's Pharaoh—no longer able to hear the cries of his own people in their enslavement.

One of Solomon's first acts was to forge an alliance with the pharaoh of Egypt by marrying his daughter. This union showcased Solomon's power and influence in the world since daughters of pharaohs rarely married outside their own family. Pharaoh's daughter was first brought to live in the City of David until Solomon's palace was completed (I Kings 3.1) then moved to a palace built just for her. This implied she was a major power player in the kingdom. Her father gave the city of Gezer as a wedding gift causing the city to became the property of Israel (I Kings 9.16), further expanding Solomon's influence.

Political marriages were a sign of great prestige in the ANE world. Solomon built alliances with the Moabites, Ammonites, Edomites, Sidonians, and Hittites through marriage—something God expressly forbade (1 Kings 11.1-6). According to the Sinai covenant, foreign wives were considered infidels and idol worshippers. *YHWH* admonished his kings against taking foreign wives. He warned of severe consequences for marrying foreigners and serving their gods; He warned His anger would be kindled against them and they would swiftly be destroyed (Deut. 7.3,4). Over time, Solomon's wives led his heart astray so that he no longer devoted himself to *YHWH* but worshipped the gods of the women he married. This resulted in the united monarchy splitting under his heir Rehoboam; centuries later, the kingdom was stripped from the House of Judah.

The sheer size of Solomon's harem seems somewhat implausible: 700 wives of nobility and 300 concubines (I Kings 11.3). In the ancient world, the harem was a status symbol that proved a ruler's great wealth. The harem's main function was to produce an heir for the kingdom. As an important civil institution, it was generally housed within the palace compound where the women of the harem and their children were given access to markets, baths, kitchens, playgrounds, and schools.

Inside the harem, the mothers often wielded power within the government. Bathsheba (granddaughter of David's councilor Ahithophel, wife of King David, and mother of King Solomon) was a political mover and shaker in her own right. She successfully blocked Adonijah's regnal aspirations by collaborating with the prophet Nathan to ensure Solomon took the throne. The book of Proverbs, written by King Solomon, outlines how to successfully govern a royal house. It is filled with wise sayings designed to bring order to the kingdom. Proverbs concludes with the description of a woman of valor, likely a reference to Bathsheba, whose wise counsel and savvy political instincts provided inspiration for the book.

Why does the Bible mention a specific number in Solomon's harem? Is 1000 a literal number? Is it hyperbole? Is it meant to be metaphorical? Could it be related to the concept of "eternal" kingship and dynasty building? The regnal years of the pre-flood patriarchs began with Adam (Gen. 5). His "years" were 930—seventy shy of 1000. Adam brought forth Seth as his heir after the death of Abel and the exile of Cain. He had other sons and daughters. Seth's regnal years were eighty-eight years short of 1000. He also had other sons and daughters. Noah produced three heirs before the flood who ruled specific regions of the ancient world. Noah's years were 950—fifty years short of 1000. Does this convey that the pre-flood patriarchs were never able to achieve the fullness of their covenantal reigns? "He remembers His covenant forever—the word He commanded for a thousand generations" (Ps. 105.8).

In a dream, Solomon asked *YHWH* for wisdom which was a typical request for kings in the ANE world. Soon after, he was called upon to judge between two women who were of one House (likely a reference to the whole House of

Israel) and who may have been part of the king's harem. Each had given birth to a son, but one of the sons had died. Both mothers insisted the living son was hers. In essence, each mother was laying claim to the throne for the son who lived. Would the heir come through Judah or through Israel? The rightful heir to Solomon's throne was Rehoboam from the House of Judah.

This parable likely foreshadowed the coming split of the united monarchy. Ongoing conflicts between the two Houses ended any hope for a return to a united kingdom. Continual religious and moral compromises led to the social disintegration of the nation. Solomon, God's human agent/ king, failed: he multiplied wives, horses, and silver and gold (Deut. 17.14-17). He had forsaken God and worshipped the idols of his wives. The fruit of Solomon's rebellion ultimately resulted in the split between the northern and southern tribes and the collapse of the kingdom many centuries later. Like the pre-flood patriarchs, Solomon also failed to fulfill his regnal destiny, but God promised to restore David's dynasty through a future heir: a Son of David.

A mysterious figure known as the King of Tyre appears in the book of Ezekiel. Compiled during the post-exilic period, Ezekiel was written to give hope to the Jews in exile in Babylon, inspiring them that they would return to the Land and rebuild the Temple. The King of Tyre is recognized for his great wisdom, wealth, and skill in trade—until his own unrighteousness makes him corrupt (Ezek. 26-28). Historically, Tyre's king is associated with Hiram I, the Phoenician King of the Sidonians (980-947) and contemporary of King David and Solomon. The city-state of Tyre was an economic center for maritime trade known for its great wealth and for the exploitation of its neighbors. It was also a center for religious idolatry and sexual immorality. Was Ezekiel's lament against the King of Tyre really a commentary on the life of King Solomon?

In modern Christian circles, the King of Tyre is generally identified as Lucifer whose name means light-bringer. A careful reading of the text, however, reveals the figure resembles Adam. Like Noah, this "Solomonic" figure is described as *tamim*: perfect or blameless. He was a king created, anointed, and enthroned on the Mountain of the Lord. "By the abundance of your trade they filled you with violence. So you have sinned. So I threw you out as a profane thing from the mountain of God... your heart was exalted because of your beauty. You corrupted your wisdom because of your splendor" (Ezek. 28.16-17).

This is just one more example of how kings become corrupt and how that corruption ultimately leads to violence. For the faithful, there is a day of reckoning coming when *YHWH* will fully restore His anointed Messiah to the throne. He is mankind's only hope for deliverance from cruel tyrants.

CHAPTER FOUR

DELIVERANCE

Let us get up early to the vineyards,
Let us see if the vine has budded,
Whether their blossoms have opened...
There I will give you my love.
Song of Songs 7.13

In ancient mythology, the land of Ararat in northern Mesopotamia was originally referred to as Urartu. The region was also first highlighted in the *Epic of Gilgamesh* as Sumeria's ancestral homeland: Aratta. Aratta featured seven mountains filled with gold, silver, lapis lazuli and other precious materials. Archaeologists and historians speculate that the Sumerians initially lived in this land once considered the cradle of civilization, the location of the Garden of Eden, and the origination of a great deluge (Vavilov 1937: 113).

According to Israel's Agricultural Research Organization, the first farming settlements were located in the region between the Tigris and the Euphrates in northeast Turkey and northern Syria. Evidence of the first domesticated crops in the area dates back about 10,000 years. Viticulture specifically began its time-honored history in the region.

The following fictional vignette about Noah incorporates historical information regarding the region in which he may have lived.

Lemech, son of Methusalah and eighth in line from Adam, moved his family to Urartu when he was fifty-six years old. The region was known for the finest grapes and wines in the world. Lemech's name (*lamed, mem, kaf*) contained a secret. By rearranging the Hebrew letters, the word *melech* (*mem, lamed, kaf*) or "king" was revealed. Viticulture was the vocation of kings who shaped their communities with respect to labor, marriage and the family.

Lemech married Betenos whose name means "House of Refuge." In the course of time, Betenos gave birth to a son, Noah—the one called by *YHWH* to bring "rest" to the earth. Lemech taught Noah the ways of the Lord, the proper protocols for entering the Divine Presence, and the agricultural arts especially regarding grape growing. After enjoying many years with his grandchildren (Ham, Shem and Japheth), Lemech died five years before a catastrophic flood hit the Fertile Crescent.

Before leaving the land by the Great Sea, Noah's ancestor Seth dug up several vines from Eden's garden for planting in the new world. Seth's was a life of dependence upon and loyalty to *YHWH*. He passed on his wisdom in the agricultural trades to prepare his lineage for a future filled with prosperity, security, and abundance. Lemech and his son Noah set out from Jerusalem with the entire clan. They traveled overland to Damascus and then to Tadmor. From Tadmor, they journeyed north to Haran before continuing on to their final destination, Lake Van, located in the mountainous region of Urartu near the headwaters of the Euphrates.

Urartu's imposing mountains created a natural barrier, protecting Lake Van from the harsh climate of the north and invading armies from the east. The tranquil environment allowed the area to become the cradle of wine production. Soon the valley would be teeming with vineyards. With his clan safely headquartered by the lake, Noah used his skills in farming and animal husbandry to build a thriving agricultural community.

The mountains of the Urartu range rose high above the grassy plains. Two craggy peaks pierced the clouds: the Greater and the Little Urartu. A profusion of streams cut through rocky outcroppings to produce a lush carpet of vegetation below. Flowers, trees, and shrubs hugged the mountainside and thrived on the valley floor. Groves of birch trees dotted the highlands, and the sweet aroma of cedar wood burst forth from the thick forests. Nearby, the headwaters of the Euphrates began as a small, narrow stream that swelled as it advanced farther south. The river cut through the highland landscape leaving behind a crooked wake as it emptied into the Tigris near Susa. The two rivers often merged only to separate again until finally flowing as one into the Persian Gulf.

The banks of the Tigris and Euphrates reminded Noah of Eden's abundant garden, fecundated by the waters of life. Urartu resembled a tri-level mountain sanctuary, and it was there Noah devoted himself to the Lord. He administered the Lord's sovereign rule on Earth through a reign of righteousness and justice.

Lake Van enjoyed a mild, pleasant climate. The land surrounding the lake was known for its rich soil and long growing season. At the base of the Urartu mountains, Noah prepared a swath of land for cultivating a vineyard. Wine production would greatly contribute to the economic stability of his family. For Noah, an agrarian lifestyle was to be valued far above urban life and its excess which existed farther south. Agricultural pursuits were synonymous with sustaining and maintaining creation—tasks connected to priestly service and kingship. There would, however, remain ongoing tensions between the rural, agrarian lifestyle and the fast-paced urban life in the city-state where mankind was busily building his own world.

Noah knew what was required for successful wine production; he was prepared for the significant and lengthy investment in time, capital, and labor. He worked tirelessly to create social and economic order. He was committed to pursuing a peace-filled environment that would guarantee patrilineal inheritance to his sons. Noah understood his responsibility for maintaining the vineyard as the family's legacy. Should Noah neglect his duties, chaos would result and his family's prosperous and peaceful existence would be cut short. The Adamic dynasty would find itself in jeopardy if he failed.

Noah built a stone altar on the side of the Little Urartu where he performed his daily priestly duties: ascending the altar to offer burnt offerings to *YHWH* and mediating on behalf of his clan. This high place was where he received *YHWH*'s instructions for maintaining order and exercising righteousness and justice in the community. Noah and his sons were also instructed by *YHWH* to build a rectangular-shaped shrine at the mountain's summit near the altar.

Noah planted the vines on newly constructed stepped terraces that provided necessary drainage for the plants. Around the terraces, he used larger stones from the loosened soil to build a retaining wall to prevent runoff. He left the smaller rocks behind to help with soil aeration and to strengthen the vine roots. He built a guard tower to monitor operations and a low wall to keep out wild animals. The greatest threat would not come from wildlife, however, but from foreign invaders attacking the vineyard and cutting off the food supply.

Hewn from rock, a winepress was constructed containing a flat surface for treading the grapes. The low walls of the press kept the juices from escaping. Treading was done by foot so as not to break the pips while the juice was being expressed. Circular vats arranged at stepped heights were connected through channels to receive the juice from the winepress. Like every other aspect of the vineyard, the location of the press was carefully chosen. A large cave nearby was ideal for storing the wine. The wine storage jars were made by local artisans who developed a unique pottery design featuring blood-red horizontal grooves running between the rim and the shoulder of the jars.

Noah worked the vineyard, watching and waiting throughout the spring and into the early days of summer as tiny, fragrant white flowers blossomed into clusters and began bearing the fruit of his labor. The brightly colored berries reached peak acidity during the hot summer months, and their flesh swelled plump and sweet. Thick, glossy leaves shaded the heavy clusters preventing them from shriveling on the vine.

As summer turned to fall and harvest time drew near, a hint of red appeared on the green leaves due to the tannins that caused the grape skins to color as they ripened. Noah and his sons searched carefully through the vine thickets for the fruit largely hidden by the oversized leaves. Finding the grapes ready for harvest, Noah signaled all able-bodied clan members to grab their pruning knives and begin cutting precisely at the shoot of the clusters. They collected the clusters and folded them gently into animal hides. They stacked hide upon hide, being careful to prevent rupture under the weight of the prolific fruit. There were only a few days left to harvest once the grapes reached their peak ripeness. Some of the more exposed grapes had already begun to ferment on the vine. The time between gathering and processing was short since the skins would break easily.

Travelers to the region often carried their wine provisions in wineskins that were much easier to transport than clay jars. Wine could be stored in old wineskins only if the fermentation process was complete. Wine that was still fermenting, or new wine, had to be poured into new wineskins since ongoing fermentation expanded the skins. An old skin had very little stretch left and was bound to explode under pressure. Old wineskins were renewed by soaking them in water until they were pliable again.

It was all hands on deck as the grapes were transferred to the winepress, which was never left unattended due to threats from pests and thieves. As clan members tread the grapes with their feet, they kept a close eye on the expressed juice as it flowed through channels into large plaster-lined vats. The frothy juice was left steaming for days before being transferred into fat-bellied storage jars with stoppers that prevented the wine from turning to vinegar. To further preserve the wine, resin was added from the terebinth tree which was a popular medicinal agent that increased the wine's beneficial properties.

The sounds of laughter and loud chatter permeated the vineyard during the harvest. It was the most joyful time of the year, and it reinforced a sense of camaraderie among the members of the clan. The laborers offered praise to *YHWH* before partaking in food and drink. Few pursuits generated such a close relationship between the people and their land as viticulture. A daily dose of wine provided much merriment and enhanced family meals and special celebrations. Festival time was particularly enjoyable for those whose lives revolved around the vineyard, as blessings to *YHWH* for creating the fruit of the vine were central. As high priest of the family, Noah passed on the special blessing for the wine: *Baruch ata Adonai, Eloheinu Melech haOlam borei pri haGafen:* Blessed are you O Lord, Our God, King of the Universe, who creates the fruit of the vine. Times of singing and dancing in the vineyard were the highlight of life in the community and were often a great time to find a wife.

Noah's reputation as a successful vintner spread throughout the Fertile Crescent. Noah walked in right standing according to the covenant of *YHWH* and showed himself blameless before the Lord. He passed on his wisdom so his sons could continue in the priestly duties of the Lord, in cultivating the earth, and in entering marriage covenants. The thrust of the community was their mission to be fruitful and multiply and to fill the earth. This was how Noah would achieve immortality. Unlike the kings of the ancient world who pursued eternal life by building monuments to themselves, undertaking massive building projects, and winning victories in legendary battles, Noah sought immortality through his descendants.

YHWH had promised Adam's seed that those who kept faith with the One True God would fulfill the eternal destiny of their forefathers.

Noah committed himself to maintaining the family vineyard. He took his role as vinedresser seriously, daily cultivating the grapes. Pruning the vines, hoeing the soil to control weeds, and repairing the infrastructure were all part of his daily regimen. Throughout the year there were ongoing tasks. He trained the vines, repaired stone walls and winepresses, and strengthened the vineyard's tower. He pruned the offshoots to concentrate growth on the main vine which helped produce consistent yields year after year. Hard pruning encouraged growth of the roots and branches, which in turn strengthened the plants. A pruning hook consisting of a sharp, concave edge attached to a wooden handle was used to cut back the thick, tough vines. This helped divert the plant's nutrients to the fruit. Pruning hooks were forged into weapons when necessary and then used again for pruning after battle.

Demand for Urartu's excellent wines exploded, particularly in southern Mesopotamia. As special envoy of Urartu, Noah was designated to lead a trade delegation down south. Meetings were scheduled with Uruk officials to discuss the purchase of Urartu wines. The demand came specifically from the ruling classes since wine was restricted to the elite and those connected to the king's royal domain. Wine was considered *the* most prestigious drink and was only available to the king's court.

Noah and his sons boarded a reed sailing boat headed for Uruk. The boat was brimming with Urartu's finest vintage. Once the vessel was cushioned with straw, casks of palm wood filled with jars of wine were carefully loaded before the rest of the cargo. Noah and his sons had prepared enough food for the weeks-long journey down river and back. There was the possibility they would need to make the arduous journey home on foot, as boats were often unable to navigate the exceptionally strong currents northward.

Noah prepared himself to meet his distant relative, Lamech, the King of Uruk (sixth generation from Cain). As the wine shipment was being off-loaded, Noah and his sons were whisked away by city officials for an audience with the king. Noah's reputation as a successful vintner had stirred the lusts of the royal court. Over the years, however, Noah had also heard of Lamech's reputation. Legends had grown concerning Cain's banishment from Eden and with it rumors of his descendants' proclivity for cruelty and wickedness. One thing Noah knew for certain: this Lamech would be nothing like his father, Lemech.

Lamech was a hunter of men who tyrannized his people. He was the first to introduce polygamy having married both Adah and Zillah. Lamech's oldest son, Jabal, pioneered the latest technologies in animal husbandry while his younger son, Jubal, revolutionized the musical arts. Tubal Cain, from his second wife, launched groundbreaking inventions in metalwork and created instruments of bronze and iron which led to an industrial transformation in the Fertile Crescent. Alongside the benefits, these technologies bolstered urbanization in the city-states and the rise of oppressive rulers.

Noah and his sons were seated directly across from Lamech's daughter Na'amah. From a young age, Na'amah had been sequestered in the king's harem in Shurrupak, awaiting marriage to a prince from the line of King Alulim. No expense was spared for this impressive, multi-course meal with wine from the vineyards of Urartu. As the evening progressed, Na'amah became fascinated with Noah's son, Ham. Ham was more than a little flattered by the attention. Noah made a mental note.

Trade negotiations continued through the night with no agreement reached. Lamech drove a hard bargain. He refused to compromise and belittled the value of Urartu's wine. He lied, manipulated, and was ultimately unwilling to meet Noah's price. Noah, for his part, refused to be bullied by this nimrod. He recognized in Lamech a corrupt, disingenuous man who could not be trusted. Noah refused to sell the clan short even as palace officials pressured him relentlessly.

Exasperated, Noah and his sons abruptly left the palace. They would have to travel back to Urartu on foot as Lamech had threatened anyone who would dare to use their boats to sail Noah and his family home. The penalty for disobedience would be a loss of livelihood or even jail time.

Being forced to travel overland meant they were unable to transport their wine back home. Noah thundered his disapproval! He warned the royal court that *YHWH* would smash the clay jars filled with wine and then similarly break the city and its leaders. Uruk officials would be forced to drink the wine of God's fury poured full strength into the cup of His wrath!

There was plenty of time to think on the journey back to Urartu. Noah and his sons spent the days talking about the state of the world they'd just seen, noting that the pull of the city-state had even reached Urartu. Once back at Lake Van, Noah focused on preserving the vineyard from the destruction he knew was coming. He dug up the grapevines Seth had given to his clan, and then he and his family of eight entered the protection of the ark-sanctuary.

The fountains of the deep burst open, water gushed from above and below, and the floodwaters submerged the land. Though chaos had returned, YHWH preserved Noah's entire family and prepared them to serve as His new creation image-bearers after the flood.

Meanwhile, the gods descended to their abode above the city of Shuruppak to make final preparations for the great flood that would destroy mankind. Inanna had her own flood event in mind, and they hurriedly gathered to circumvent her. Having been humiliated when the former King of Uruk desecrated her precious garden, Inanna was now ready to unleash her full fury on the land between the rivers. To counter, the gods cast lots. Enki was chosen to head up the heavenly council. He recommended assigning a human representative along with his family to ride out the flood.

Instructions were passed on to the last of the antediluvian kings, King Ubara-tutu of Shuruppak, who was told to tear down Alulim's summer house to build a boat/sanctuary from reeds. He was to build it in the shape of a cube with seven levels. Most importantly, he was to caulk the sanctuary with bitumen and leave behind his possessions. His mission was to save his family.

A menacing silence spread throughout the cosmos as a suffocating mist removed all signs of light. The gods opened the windows of heaven and released the floodgates. Safely ensconced in their temple tower, they watched without remorse as the first streams of water swirled in the sky before falling to the ground. Floodwaters burst forth from the lakes and rivers, springs and canals, fracturing the land as if it were a brittle clay pot.

It had been an unseasonably warm spring in Sumer. As dawn delivered a cloudless morning, the inhabitants of the alluvial plains scurried about attending to their daily routines. Without warning, thick dark clouds rolled in from the east overwhelming the clear blue skies. As the clouds grew thicker, darker, and angrier, a sense of foreboding gripped the hearts of the people.

Farther north, clouds threatened the Greater Urartu. Water poured from a heavenly spout onto the peaks of the Urartu range; streams rushed down through the mountain's crevices, swirling and gushing, until they reached the headwaters of the Euphrates. The water was like a wall of cement crushing everything in its path. The roar was deafening as it continued downstream overflowing river banks and wiping out the cities of Sumer.

The Euphrates continued to rise above her banks, flooding the entire region. It was a catastrophe that led to the death of masses of humanity, the ruin of all Sumer's houses and businesses, and the complete destruction of agricultural land, animals, and livelihoods. The excess rainfall caused dams to break and mudslides to envelope the entire landscape.

The raging waters grabbed large pieces of earth from the river banks, dragging them down into the already muddied waters. Heavy rains swamped tributaries. Sand, silt, and leaves clogged irrigation channels until they overflowed. Waves at a height never seen carried the waterlogged debris. The raging torrents pushed through the city streets. Mountains of sand buried homes. Flash flooding created a destructive soup that intensified as the rains continued to fall. Entire towns were submerged—crops destroyed, trees uprooted, houses washed away, cattle drowned. As water levels continued rising, those left alive evacuated to higher ground but soon ran out of places of safety.

After a significant amount of time, the rain ceased. A thick layer of silt lay like a yellow blanket, wet and heavy, suffocating the city of Shuruppak. Shuruppak proved to be ground zero for the deluge, but layers of riverine sediments extended as far north as the city of Kish—whose hegemony would rise after the flood. The Shuruppak flood, as it came to be known, was the result of a perfect storm: the damming of the Karun River, the flooding of the Tigris and the Euphrates, and an unprecedented snow melt in the Greater Urartu.

Up north, two enormous volcanic cones appeared on the Urartu horizon. The mountains became a debris field covered in basalt. New peaks rose forming steep, rugged slopes that stretched nearly 17,000 ft above the valley floor below. The mountains, once covered with a bounty of green forests, were barren. No one had survived. In the distance, a wooden box was hidden away, covered in mud and frozen to the snow-capped mountains of the Greater Urartu.

Once the floodwaters had receded, Noah's family exited the ark. Noah, tools in hand, set off to examine the extent of the damage. To his amazement, he discovered several perfectly intact vines loaded with clusters of grapes.

The Reed Boat

Southern Mesopotamia's earliest reed boats have been dated to the Ubaid period (c. 5500 BCE). These small-masted crafts were a boon to the local economy making commercial trading possible between villages up and down the Tigris and Euphrates. The boats were constructed from a type of tall reed grass called phragmites that was first used to build reed-hut shrines. The boats featured square sails made from cloth and lattice ropes that stretched across the hull and the masts. Like Noah's ark, these boats were coated with a special mixture of bitumen, pitch, and oil for waterproofing (Gen. 6.14).

Oppenheim explains that the ideal ANE temple was based on the primeval reed-hut shrine which played a central role in ancient myths. Later temples revealed an aquatic past and commonality with Noah's ark as reed shrines atop sea-faring vessels. Oppenheim ties the origins of the reed-hut shrine to naval processions that sailed the Tigris and Euphrates from one temple to another (1944: 54).

ANE flood heroes acquired their boat building materials from dismantled reed-huts that had once served as sanctuaries. Both Utnapishtim (Babylonian flood myth) and Atrahasis (Akkadian flood myth) received divine communications while at their god's reed-hut. A quote from *Gilgamesh XI* shows the value of these shrines: "Far-sighted Ea swore the oath [of secrecy] with them, so he repeated their speech to a reed hut, reed hut, reed hut, brick wall, brick wall, listen, reed hut and pay attention, brick wall: Man of Shuruppak, son of Ubara-tutu, dismantle your house, build a boat" (Dalley 1991: 110). The primeval, reed-hut shrine was initially an oracle from which the deity communicated and maintained cultic connections between Heaven and Earth.

A Sumerian custom related to human burial involved laying the body in the reeds of Enki, Lord of the Earth. Enki would sit in his rectangular-shaped reed sanctuary after a corpse was placed inside. The reed-hut boat would then be floated downstream. "Throughout history, the center for the worship of Enki in Eridu was the reed hut, even though it was surrounded by other very impressive temples. The reed-hut functioned as the original temple and despite technological advances, it remained at the core of their religious beliefs" (Coppens 2004).

In Egypt, the reed boat was constructed from papyrus that was cultivated from the banks of the Nile River. Bundles of grass were tied together in a way that trapped air inside the reeds to provide buoyancy. The tighter the binding the better. These bundles of grass allowed the boats to sit high in the water, sinking only if they became waterlogged. The sails were made from the skins of the papyrus stem which were twisted and braided into rope that secured the lines. Woven reed mats were stitched into the hull then supported by additional lines to keep the bundles from buckling. The hull was waterproofed with a coating of pitch (Is. 18.2).

Archaeology connects reed shrines to ritual boats at the time of Egypt's New Kingdom. The Egyptians believed the sun traveled across the sky in a papyrus boat. The concept of a reed-hut as a temple is a view supported by many scholars (McCann 2013: 131). First identified as a sacred shrine, the reed-hut was central in most Egyptian temples and became a powerful religious symbol for their mythology (David 2017: 8-9).

The word for ark, *tevah*, is the same used for Moses' reed "basket." *Tevah* ˋcan be translated as holy shrine, box, chest, or coffin. *Tevah* can also refer to a large building, such as a palace, and in the Old Kingdom it referred to a shrine. Some scholars see *tevah* as a word loaned from the Egyptian language that eventually became connected to the Ark of the Covenant in Mishnaic Hebrew. The chest as a holy shrine was common in Egyptian temples. (As an interesting side-note, the letters in *tevah* can also be rearranged to form the word *ha'beit*, which means house.)

A simple Egyptian *tevah* was an elongated chest with a small door in the front upper portion. During festivals, this chest was a key part of ritual aquatic processions down the Nile River and was set afloat from one temple to another. This suggests the *tevah* was given special status as a maritime vehicle for the gods (especially the sun god Re or the god of the afterlife Osiris) and that it housed their images. In the Egyptian tradition, the term *tevah* was never used for a ship (Yahuda 1933: 262). Kenneth Kitchen adds that these maritime temples were considered private residences for the gods.

Noah's ark, whether in the Mesopotamian or the Egyptian tradition, was likely patterned after the popular reed-hut shrine. The main distinction, of course, was its sheer size! The ark was gargantuan compared to the average reed-hut at the time. *YHWH* used Noah's ark to deconstruct the world of the gods by diminishing the size of their temples. Noah's sanctuary-box encompassed the cosmos. The world beyond its hull was a perversion of the natural order and a place of instability. Inside Noah's ark resided a living, human image-bearer of *YHWH*.

God told Noah to construct an ark of gopherwood, to make "rooms," and to smear it inside and out with pitch (Gen. 6.14). Morales suggests the second element in this list should be translated "reeds," not rooms (2012: 147). Reed boats were smeared inside and out with pitch to prevent leaking. (Pitch is from the Hebrew *kapar* which means to cover and has the same root for atonement).

In *Gilgamesh XI.1* and *Atrahasis III.2*, the list of materials is the same: wood timbers, reeds, and pitch. The Hebrew word *kinnim* is generally translated rooms although its root, *kanah*, means stalk or reed. *Ken* or *kanan* is a bird's nest made from reed stalks. Jewish mystical writings tie the bird's nest to the Garden of Eden and also to the Temple where the Messiah will be hidden while awaiting his coronation. "Then the Messiah will arise from the Garden of Eden, from that place which is called 'The Bird's Nest' " (*Zohar*, Soncino Press 2:8a). Israel is often compared to a mother bird, the dove, who will return to her nest, the Temple. And of course, the dove in the Noah narrative returns to the ark with an olive leaf in her beak.

Morales adds that "reed" could also be an allusion to the menorah since reeds, *kinnim*, refer to the menorah's shaft and branches (2012: 147). If Noah's ark was an early reed boat shrine, it likely functioned as a temple—a ritual place for sacrifice later realized in Jerusalem's Temple. In the mythological world of the Egyptians and the Mesopotamians, Noah's reed boat would be recognized as a divine shrine. More importantly, Noah's ark represented a renewed cosmos—a place for the Divine Presence—a re-creation of the once contaminated cosmic House.

The miraculous deliverance of Moses from the Nile River shares elements with creation. Pharaoh decreed every Hebrew male child be thrown into the river: the place of judgment, death, and chaos, and the domain ruled by the gods. Moses was discovered by Pharaoh's daughter as he was floating in a reed-hut shrine on the waters of the Nile. His *tevah* fluttered over the waters like a bird hovers over its nest. At the beginning of creation, darkness was on the face of the *tehom*, the deep, which some scholars link to the waters of chaos and the disorder the gods epitomized before creation (Gen. 1.1-3). Here in Exodus, God is deconstructing Pharaoh's rule. Pharaoh was the incarnation of the gods who controlled the seas, and he would ultimately drown in the very domain he ruled over—the *tehom*, the chaotic deep of *Yam Suph*, the Sea of Reeds (Ex. 15).

Pharaoh's decision to kill the sons and save the daughters was undermined by the women who saved Moses (the midwives, Moses's mother, and Pharaoh's daughter). Their collective act of "civil disobedience" was in direct violation to Pharaoh's policy of death. The midwives resisted Pharaoh's command to drown the Hebrew baby boys by delivering Moses on the birthing stool. This was an intentional, subversive act against Pharaoh's decree. Through them, creation was restored, new life came forth, and a savior was born who would later rescue his people by liberating them from Egyptian bondage. God's creational order was realized through these women whose defiance was symbolic of new creation and the birthing process.

In Scripture, creation is inextricably linked to women giving birth: Eve is the mother of the living. Women are called the House of their husbands responsible to protect and preserve their seed. The House of the Sanctuary, *Beit HaMikdash*, is feminine. The Kingdom of God, *Malchut Shemayim*, is feminine. The Temple served as the spiritual nest for mankind. Rashi stated that the bird is the community of

Israel who will find its nest when the Temple is rebuilt. "The throne of Glory stood suspended in the air hovering above the surface of the waters by the breath of the mouth of the Holy One – just as a dove hovers over its nest" (Babylonian Talmud, Chaggigah 15a).

Pharaoh's chosen instrument of destruction, the waters of chaos, was the very thing God used to save Moses. Through Moses' birth and salvation from death, God was deconstructing the gods of this world through a new creation event that had cosmic significance. Fretheim sees yet another correlation between Moses's birth and creation in that Moses's mother conceived and bore a son and saw that he was "good" (Ex. 2.2). Good is connected to creational order; the light at creation was "good" (Fretheim 2010: 31-38, 268-289). Israel's savior, Moses, would defeat the gods of Egypt and set the captives free to form a new creation nation. We find God upending the world's disorder to institute His creational order.

Pharaoh's daughter saved Moses from the judgment of the gods. Jochebed (Yah is Glory) took a *tevah* of papyrus reeds and coated it with tar and pitch. Then she placed her infant son inside the *tevah* and laid it in the reeds by the banks of the Nile (Ex. 2.3)—likely at a location commonly used by royalty. The *tevah* for Moses resembled a reed shrine designed to carry the image of one of Egypt's Nile gods. What must Pharaoh's daughter have thought when she found it?

Moses's story may be a historical reworking of a popular Egyptian myth detailing the "miraculous" birth of the god Horus. Was this myth being transformed to align with God's revelation of Himself? Horus, whose name means "the one far above," was also hidden away at birth and placed in a reed-hut at the edge of the Nile River. There, he was protected from his Uncle Seth (the god of storms, chaos, and war) who became jealous of his brother Osiris (primeval king of Egypt) and murdered him by cutting him into pieces. Osiris's wife, Isis, restored the body of Osiris which enabled them to conceive a son, Horus. Like Moses, Horus was nursed by his mother after being rescued from the river (Rendsburg 2006: 204-205).

Horus avenged his father's death by casting Seth into the desert beyond Egypt. His triumph over Seth restored balance to the world allowing Horus to claim rulership. Once enthroned, Horus served as the protector of the Pharaoh. This entire event became central to kingship, succession, and social order in Egypt. Horus was depicted as a falcon-headed god with a double crown and Pharaoh took on Horus's mantle as his earthly embodiment established to restore cosmic and social order. The casting out of Seth was celebrated at festival times throughout the year.

What did Pharaoh's daughter expect to see inside the *tevah*, the reed shrine, as she opened it? It is clear from the text that she knew she'd found one of the Hebrew babies. Did she see Moses as being related in some way to the living incarnation of the god Horus? Did she understand this baby was the Son of *YHWH*? Did she recognize her role in rescuing the living image of the living God from an Egyptian shrine? Once again, *YHWH* was deconstructing the world of the Egyptian gods through Moses's birth and deliverance from water. Pharaoh's daughter came face to face with the living image of the invisible God, not the substitute image of her father's god.

A similar story is told of Sargon I, King of Akkad and founder of the Mesopotamian empire. A priestess who had taken a vow of chastity became pregnant, and she was forced to bear the child in secret. She placed the child in a "basket" in the reeds along the river's edge where he was discovered by a water drawer who then raised him as his own. The goddess Ishtar protected the child and made him King of Akkad.

"I am the great ruler the mighty king of Akkad. My mother was low-born; I never knew my father...after I was conceived, my mother had to keep my existence hidden: she gave birth to me in secret. She placed me in a basket of reed, the gaps caulked up with tar: So when she consigned me to the waters of the river, I was not overwhelmed but floated. The current carried me along to where Akki, the water carrier found me. He reared me as his own son and subsequently made me his gardener. The goddess Ishtar loved me" (*Legend of Sargon*, 11.11-13).

Moses's story culminates in Israel's release from Egyptian captivity as the nation was led by God to the Sea of Reeds. Though rendered "Red Sea" in our English Bibles, *Yam Suph* is better translated as Sea of Reeds. *Suph* are the reeds at the edge of a stream, canal, or river bank (Ex. 2.3). *Yam* is the god of the sea who is portrayed as a dragon and creator of chaos. From a post-exilic perspective, Israel would have interpreted *YHWH*'s splitting of *Yam Suph* as His victory over *Yam*. When Israel crossed the sea on dry ground, the nation was transformed through a new creation event. Just as He'd done at creation, *YHWH* conquered the forces of chaos. He exercised control over the seas to give Israel the victory over Pharaoh and the gods of Egypt. God was clearly deconstructing a popular ANE myth as well as upending the dark powers of that world.

Aaru means reeds or rushes and in Egyptian mythology is connected to the Field of Reeds: the heavenly paradise where Osiris ruled. It was the Egyptian version of a paradisiacal afterlife where agricultural work continued. The Field of Reeds was a set of islands located in the middle of flowing rivers. It was considered a place of eternal pleasure. Getting there required a long and perilous journey filled with many traps. To enter Aaru, one passed through fifteen gates guarded by demons armed with knives. Aaru was located in the east where the sun rises, whereas the Holy of Holies in the Temple was located in the west where the sun set.

According to some creation myths, the first object to rise from the waters of chaos was a reed—a symbol of longevity and immortality. Reeds designated a place of high culture and ancient wisdom—heaven's doorway. This was the place where the soul passed to the afterlife. How fitting that Pharaoh drowned in the Sea of Reeds! This would have undoubtedly spoken to Israel that *YHWH* was the most powerful. They saw with their own eyes that it is *YHWH* who determines when and where the immortal soul will rest and not the gods of this world.

Ark And Tabernacle

Noah's ark served as a sacred space for the Divine Presence. It was a place set apart in the cosmos where God preserved Noah and his family. It also served as a bulwark against a world consigned to destruction. Kline describes Noah's three-storied miniature cosmos as a refuge from evil, claiming that when it rested on Mount Ararat it became "the temple of the new creation—a kind of primeval Zion" (2006: 87-90).

Morales sees the ark as a microcosm within the cosmos, a ritual model of creation complete with its own humanity (2017: 8). The ark replicated elements of creation. It was fashioned as a cosmic house that functioned as a mini-world filled with living creatures (2015: 152). Noah replayed the role of Adam in the garden—peacefully abiding with the animals in paradise. Sarna writes, "Noah's ark is the matrix of a new creation, and, like Adam in the garden of Eden, he [Noah] lives in harmony with the animals" (2001: 50). The Messianic Age is generally viewed through the lens of eschatology, but it also points back to creation, the garden, and Noah's ark where the wolf dwells with the lamb, the leopard lies down with the kid, and the calf is unafraid of the lion. Life inside the ark exemplified the harmony of the original cosmic house (Is. 11:6-9).

Levenson sees a similar relationship between creation and the construction of the Mosaic Tabernacle which functioned in much the same way (1994: 85-86). Like the ark, it was a miniature mobile cosmos, and like the ark it was designed as a replica of the three-story universe: a cosmic city-temple of God. "Established in Sabbatical rest on the Ararat mountaintop, the ark was a redemptive restoration of the mountain of God in Eden, itself a replica of the heavenly Zaphon [to hide]" (Kline (1996: 216). Josephus saw the Tabernacle as a reflection of the cosmos (*Antiquities of the Jews* 3.123-50). Morales attributes the same to Noah's ark in that it was a cosmos in miniature—a substitute refuge while the cosmos was being cleansed (2015: 59).

Waltke notes that, as the sanctuary of Israel, the Tabernacle represented a small, idealized island of order in a world threatened on all sides by the chaos of a dangerous wilderness environment. In the same way, Noah's ark was a sacred place of order that preserved those inside from the chaotic waters outside: "A place that preserved equilibrium for God's presence which in turn was an anchor against disorder" (quoted in Morales 2012: 159 notes *Structure of Leviticus* 2001: 296). The ark provided a type of exodus from the destructive waters (the nations) with the birth of a new cosmic creation (161). Sailhammer connects the deliverance of Noah and his family with Israel's Exodus from Egypt.

According to Kline, the ark wasn't just a picture of the restoration of the kingdom to its "primeval paradise condi-tion." Rather, "it symbolically portrayed the kingdom as a culture-urban structure, at last brought to perfection. The ark encapsulated the city of God...[a prophetic type] of royal temple, the house of God. It is the final eschatological mani-festation of the Creator's cosmic house of heaven and earth, which was typified by Israel's microcosmic tabernacle and temple" (2000: 225-226). Kline's description of the ark as an urban structure brings to mind Revelation's Holy city, the New Jerusalem, the Tabernacle of God coming down from Heaven. The New Jerusalem, found to be 12,000 stadia square, is measured with a "reed staff" (Rev. 21.16).

Scholars debate whether Noah's ark was of Mesopotamian or Egyptian origin. In his book, *The Divine Warrior*, Michael Homan explains that, like the ark, the Egyptian war camp (13th C. BCE) was rectangular (Mesopotamian camps were laid out in an oval). These rectangular camps were oriented eastward as was the wilderness Tabernacle and its courtyard. Pharaoh's tent, located in the heart of the war compound, was a two-chambered, rectangular structure like the Tabernacle. "[The] inner chamber or throne room of the pharaoh's tent strongly resembles the plan of the Tabernacle's Holy of Holies. Images of the winged god Horus flanked the pharaoh's cartouche, much as the winged cherubim covered *YHWH's* Tabernacle throne" (Homan 2000: 29).

The similarities between the Tabernacle and Noah's ark suggest that the writer of Genesis was intentionally connecting them. Morales writes extensively about this in his book, *The Tabernacle Prefigured*, making the case that the ark prefigures or foreshadows the wilderness Tabernacle. Westermann explains that, "The place where God allows His glory to appear is the place whence the life of the people is preserved. The ark corresponded to this in the primeval event where the concern is for the preservation of humanity and what it saves is natural creation…the parallel between the ark and the tabernacle has a profound meaning" (1974: 421).

Fretheim also connects the two: "Both ark and tabernacle are commanded by God, whose precise directions are communicated to the human leader, who proceeds to carry out the directions in obedient detail" (2010: 268-269). Noah and Moses found favor in God's sight and did all the Lord had commanded them (Gen. 6.22, 7.5; Ex. 39.42, 40.16). Fretheim sees the ark as a temple structure similar in construction to those found in Mesopotamia. The floodwaters and the wilderness are the two most prominent symbols for chaos in the Old Testament. The Tabernacle and ark are portable sanctuaries, one on the sea and one on land, both carrying people through chaos (268-269).

Though modern readers equate the ark with a seafaring vessel, many scholars have concluded that, from an ANE perspective, Noah's ark was never intended to be a ship. Sarna explains that the ark is a chest-like vessel without rudder, sail, navigational aid, or crew (1970: 49). The ark is described as a vast enclosed chest designed for housing and preserving a large number of living creatures. Keil and Delitzsch explain that it is probable, "the ark was built in the form not of a ship, but of a chest, with a flat bottom, like a floating house, as it was not meant for sailing, but merely to float upon the water..." Others have also noted that the box-like craft had no rudder or sail, no oars or navigational aid. Cassuto explains the Genesis narrative refers to a structural shape, not a ship, and that the ark is something that floats on the surface of the waters and moves in accordance with the thrust of the water and wind (1961: 60).

Creation architecture divides the world into compartments or rooms for habitation. The sky was made as a roof for the earth and lights were installed for illumination (Currid 1997: 43). "As in the case of other replicas of the heavenly sanctuary, like the tabernacle and temple as well as the visible cosmos, so in the case of his ark-house it was God who provided the architectural plans" (Kline 2006: 87).

Wenham points out that if each deck were divided into three sections, the ark would have three decks the same height as the Tabernacle and three sections on each deck the same as the Tabernacle courtyard (1987: 174). Both ark and Tabernacle exhibit a tripartite structure that aligns with an ANE cosmic three-decked world and mountain: Heaven, Earth and Sea/Underworld (Lambert, *The cosmology of Sumer and Babylon*: 42-65). The ark was built as a mobile mountain sanctuary with a three-decked design: "You shall make it with lower, second, and third" (Gen. 6.16). In Scripture, Mount Sinai is portrayed as a three-tiered vertical structure: Moses in a cloud on top of the mountain, the elders part way up the mountain, and the people near the base of the mountain. *Yeshua* refers to his Father's House as having many rooms/mansions where he is going to prepare a place, all in the context of a cosmic temple (Jn. 14.2).

With the Tabernacle and the ark, there is an emphasis on mobility. The ark is moving over the face of the waters, paralleling the Spirit in the creation account. The Tabernacle is moving through the wilderness landscape and, according to Cassuto, is a miniature, portable Mount Sinai (1967: 316,484). Fretheim sees "striking parallels" between the Tabernacle and Noah's ark in that both are viewed as a "means by which the people of God can move in a secure and ordered way beyond apostasy and through a world of disorder on their way to a new creation" (1996: 238).

As a floating sanctuary, the ark was a mobile temple that covered the whole earth. This alludes to the kingdom expanding to the four corners of the world. Noah's ark resembled the Ark of the Covenant that was housed inside the Holy of Holies of the Tabernacle. This chest-shaped box represented *YHWH's* portable chariot throne and was carried by the priests with poles as they traveled from camp to camp. Ezekiel (1) describes God's mobile throne as immense "wheels within wheels" transporting four living creatures who each resemble a winged man with four faces and who move together as the Spirit moves. Noah's three-decked ark symbolized a temple that functioned as a *mobile* shrine moving over the waters of chaos—a vehicle of rescue after which God's portable pavilion or chariot was designed (Morales 2012: 152). The Tabernacle served a similar function.

Both the Tabernacle and the ark were inaugurated on the first day of the first month of Nisan (Aviv), which was the annual New Year's Day of the festival/agricultural calendar (in the Second Temple period). "And it came to pass in the six hundred and first year, in the first month, the first day of the month, that the waters were dried up from the earth; and Noah removed the covering of the ark" (Gen. 8.13 NKJV). "On the first day of the first month you shall set up the tabernacle of the tent of meeting" (Ex 40.2). *YHWH's* mobile sanctuaries were both dedicated on the first day of Israel's liturgical year.

As the waters "strengthened," Noah's ark rose fifteen cubits above the mountains (Gen. 7.20). A wall of curtains fifteen cubits in length flanked the entrance to the Tabernacle (Ex. 27.14-15, 38.14). In the Temple, fifteen curved steps led up to the great Nicanor Gate at the east side of the Court of Israel (Josephus *Wars of the Jews* 5). The number fifteen is related to the worship of *YHWH* at its highest level when entering the Presence of God. As the pilgrims ascended the mountain to celebrate their festivals in Jerusalem, they sang the fifteen Songs of Ascent (Ps. 120-134). The fifteen words of the Aaronic Benediction (Num 6.22-27), spoken by the priests in the temple courtyard, were a blessing upon the nation of Israel.

Finally, a connection is made between the forty days of rain in the flood story and the forty years Israel wandered in the wilderness. Ark and Tabernacle both represented the center of God's Presence on Earth and provided a refuge in the exilic environment of sea and wilderness, with forty representing the natural world order.

Noah Is Rest

Heaven is my throne, and earth is my footstool.
Where is the house that you will build me?
And where is the place of my rest.

ISAIAH 66.1

God saw the earth and it had rotted because all flesh had become morally corrupted, following their own way (Gen. 6.12). Noah, however, was a righteous man, blameless in his generation and one who continually walked with God (Gen. 6.9). He was *tzadik*. *Tzadik* is righteous in a legal sense: innocent or acquitted, one whose conduct is pure, and who is in right standing in the covenant. He was *tamim* meaning blameless in a cultic sense: whole or complete like the clean animals used for the offerings. He walked (*halach*) according to God's commandments.

Noah was the priest/king who could ascend the mountain and enter the Divine Presence for worship; he was a new Adam in a newly created world. He could enter the paradisiacal Holy of Holies. "And he [Noah] knew that the Garden of Eden is the Holy of Holies, and the dwelling place of the Lord, and Mount Sinai the centre of the desert, and Mount Zion—the navel of the earth: these three were created as holy places facing each other" (*Jubilees* 8.19). He was the "new born" king, heir to *YHWH's* throne, who would eradicate evil, act on behalf of the weak and oppressed, and establish righteousness and justice—essential for a reigning king. "Righteousness and justice are the foundation of Your throne" (Ps. 89.15). This golden age of creation would be short-lived.

Noach (Noah), from the Hebrew root *Nuach*, means rest, order, or peace. Rest is enthronement language with the king's role being primarily to maintain order in the world. Brueggemann says Noah functioned as a type of royal priestly figure. Noah brought "rest" to the earth. He was the new Adam in replaying the creation story. He was humanity's representative mediating between Heaven and Earth. Like Moses would, he led his family out of chaos to the stability of the mountain. He rebuilt the cosmos for *YHWH's* presence, ruled over the earth, and cultivated a garden vineyard. He was a savior, deliverer, and preserver of his family's seed until he, like Adam, allowed the sacred space to become corrupt.

After exiting the ark, Noah built an altar and gave an offering to the Lord from the clean animals aboard the ark. The clean animals were designated for the altar. They supplied food for the priestly class as part of the cultic service rather than providing a new diet for mankind (Gen. 7.2,8; Lev. 11.47). As *Adonai* smelled the soothing aroma of the burnt offering, the estrangement between God and Adam was reversed. Wenham sees a direct relationship between Noah's burnt offering, called the daily elevation offering, and the offerings of the Levitical priests.

There are other cultic elements which relate to the ark as a sanctuary. One in particular is based on the wordplay between *gopher* (wood) and *kaphar* (pitch). Rich cultic overtones are presented in the word *kaphar* as a ransom with its half-shekel temple atonement and with *kapporet*, the throne cover (mistakenly referred to as the mercy seat). *Kippur*, from the root *kaphar*, means atone. The high priest entered the Holy of Holies on *Yom Kippur*, the Day of Atonement to atone for his own family and the nation. Priestly rituals of atonement involved smearing or wiping blood on the altar; a similar movement was required in applying pitch to the ark.

Scholars have long pondered why Noah "profaned" the vineyard, got drunk on the wine he produced, and exposed his nakedness: "And profaned the man of the earth and he planted a vineyard. He drank some of the wine, got drunk, and was uncovered in his tent" (Gen. 9:20,21). Elsewhere in Scripture, *Adonai* says, "I will profane (*chalil*) My Sanctuary, the pride of your might, the desire of your eyes and the longing of your soul" (Ezek. 24.21).

Profane is the Hebrew word *chalil*, which means to open or pierce. Today, profane has a negative connotation. Anciently, it simply identified that which was common or public. Common referred to everyday life while holy referred to the ritual, ceremonial life within the sacred space. Holy things were set apart for a specific function and purpose. For a common element to become holy, it must be transferred to God's realm and dedicated to Him. Holiness increases as the person or thing comes in closer proximity to God. Therefore, holiness is connected to ritual status, not human behavior.

There is the possibility that Noah allowed the status of the vineyard to become common and that it was no longer dedicated to *YHWH*. If Noah was functioning as a priest in the sacred space, drinking the wine should have been part of the cultic ritual, not an over-indulgence due to a hard day in the vineyard. Did allowing the sacred space to become common change the ceremonial function of the wine? In the book of Jubilees, Noah was a priest who made atonement for the corrupted earth and maintained the laws of cultic purity in the sacred space. Did Noah pollute the sacred space by making it common? If so, God would have no other option but to abandon the vineyard sanctuary by removing His Presence.

And Noah's nakedness? Was this the consequence for defiling the holiness of the sacred space and making it common? Nakedness was often a euphemism for exile. For one to lay down naked implied that they were without armor and outer robes and were an easy target for the enemy.

Outside the sacred space boundary, the priests wore ordinary clothes. Inside, vestments worn by the priests matched the areas of the Temple to which they had access. Each time the high priest moved from one level of holiness to another, he changed his clothes which also marked a change in status. On *Yom Kippur*, he changed clothes five times when he entered the Holy of Holies.

Adam and Eve served as priests and were granted access to Eden where they wore garments of celestial light (*Zohar*, II, 229a-b). Once they broke covenant and transgressed the laws of the sacred space, they were stripped of their "angelic" garments and were naked, having put on mortal flesh. *YHWH*, in his mercy, clothed them with a *ketonet* of skins. A *ketonet* is a long-sleeved garment (Joseph's robe was a *ketonet* not a multi-colored coat). Oppenheim, in his book *The Golden Garments of the Gods*, describes a *ketonet passim* (a long-sleeved robe with sleeves reaching to the palm of the hands) as a ceremonial robe sewn with gold ornaments used to dress images of royalty.

In the garden, Adam and Eve sewed aprons of fig leaves to cover their nakedness. In the vineyard, Noah's children Shem and Japheth covered his nakedness with an outer garment. The removal of his priestly garments represented the shame of exile and a lower level of sanctity outside the camp. Was this a message to the exiles in Babylon that defiling the Holy Temple in Jerusalem and polluting the land had led to their exile? Was the writer of Genesis revealing that after the flood mankind *returned* to a place of exile—cast out from God's sacred space?

The climax of Noah and the flood story is found in the phrase "Then God Remembered Noah" (Gen. 8.1). This phrase is at the center of a chiastic structure (Gen. 6.5 to 8.21 is one example). In the ancient world, "to remember" meant to bring something into existence—to give it life and identity. This statement confirmed God's promise to Noah and his progeny, and ultimately to Israel, that He will protect, preserve, and return His seed from exile and into the Presence of God who will dwell in a new creation temple.

After Noah, next in line was Abraham who was called from Ur of Chaldees to move westward toward the Holy of Holies. He was called to restore the covenant and to sanctify God's sanctuary. Abraham declared his allegiance to God, and it was credited to him as right standing in the covenant.

CHAPTER FIVE

RE-CREATION

For the vineyard of *Adonai Tzv'aot* is
the House of Israel, and the people of
Judah the planting of His delight.
Isaiah 5.7

The New Creation Vineyard

At creation, *YHWH* planted a garden; after the flood,
Noah planted a vineyard (Gen. 9.20). The establishment of
gardens/vineyards epitomized creational order. The fruit
of the vine was God's sustenance to His people. "Behold,
I create new heavens and a new earth... be glad and rejoice
forever in what I am creating... then I will rejoice in Jerusalem and be glad in my people... They will build houses and
inhabit them, they will plant vineyards and eat their fruit"
(Is. 65:17-21).

Grapes were a luxury crop requiring an investment of time. Planting a vineyard indicated both a sense of permanency and stability for the nation. "When they reached as far as the Valley of Eschol, [the spies] cut a single branch with a cluster of grapes. It was carried on a pole between them..." (Num. 13:23). Viticulture made an indelible mark on Israelite culture, and wine proved to be one of the most important food products as, in addition to other benefits, it offered relief from the curse of toil in the world (Eccl. 9.7).

Cultivating the earth was priestly work. The purpose of cultivation was to elevate humanity with wine and thus vineyards represented the pinnacle of God's covenantal blessing. Pruning, hoeing, and fertilizing were all considered priestly duties—daily work necessary to produce a good crop and to make the sacred space glorious. The people beautified the Lord's vineyard through acts of worship to their king who was *YHWH's* choice vine. In the ANE, cultivated vineyards were associated with kingship; a fruitful vineyard revealed a well-managed royal garden and by extension a well-managed empire. In Mesopotamian royal ideology, "gardener" was a stock title for the king in his kingdom (Barker 2010: 434).

In the ANE, wine production operated under state control. It was restricted to the royal domain and centered around the king, specifically in Mesopotamia. Wine was kept from the common people. The palace reliefs of King Sennacherib of Assyria featured vines and vineyards. In Egypt, vineyards functioned almost exclusively under a temple's governing authority.

The reigns of the eighth-century BCE rulers, Jeroboam II of Israel and Uzziah of Judah (two of the most powerful kings to rule since Solomon), were the backdrop for Isaiah's parable of the vineyard (5.1-7; 27.2-5). Assyria's dominance in the region was legendary, and under the reign of Tiglath Pileser III (745-727 BCE) its territory was now expanded toward Israel and Judah. The Assyrian king created mini vassal states governed by handpicked officials, and he deported those in the upper classes to other parts of the empire in order to maintain tight control.

Judah and Israel had been enjoying a rather cosmopolitan lifestyle. Trade flourished, which brought prosperity to the urban upper classes. As economic circumstances vastly improved, the people began to indulge in all manner of idolatry. Israel's newfound prosperity did not escape the notice of Tiglath Pileser who forced her citizens to pay tribute to the Assyrian empire. The wealthy oppressed the poor in an effort to recover their financial losses. The burden of increased taxes and land expropriations fell mostly on the lower classes and those in rural communities. Struggling farmers were assessed according to crop production, while drought forced many to sell family lands and leave their homes as indentured servants. The wealthy were tone deaf to the needs of the poor and oppressed. Jerusalem's vineyards were eventually threatened by King Sennacherib (701 BCE) whose envoy Rabshakeh offered to spare the grape crop if Jerusalem's inhabitants surrendered (Is. 36.16-17). Vineyard destruction, as it turns out, was a favorite pastime of ancient armies. "Many shepherds ruined my vineyard. They trampled my property. They made my pleasant portion a desolate wilderness" (Jer. 12.10).

Isaiah's parable speaks of the condition of the heart of God's people and their king. The once faithfulJerusalem had become a harlot filled with injustice, immorality, and drunkenness. Her rulers acted like children, her people oppressed one another, and she was overrun with idols. *YHWH* promised the ruling elites that he would strip them of their finery and expose their nakedness. He had expected good grapes, but the vineyard yielded only worthless ones (Is. 5.2b,4b). The vineyard of *Adonai* had been corrupted by the nation's leadership. "I had planted you as a choice vine from completely faithful seed. How then did you become to Me a wandering wild vine" (Jer. 2.21)?

The central vine in the vineyard was the noblest of all plants and represented the king (Barker 2014: 425). "The scepter will not pass from Judah, nor the ruler's staff from between his feet, until he to whom it belongs will come... Binding his foal to the vine, his donkey's colt to the choice vine, he washes his garments in wine, and in the blood of grapes his robe" (Gen. 49.10-11). The Bible is filled with poetic metaphors related to vines, vineyards, and wine; the earth is compared to a vineyard (Rev. 14.19), and blood is compared to the juice of grapes (Ezek. 19.10; Matt. 26.28). Pruning hooks, knives, and sickles are tools used for judgment (Is. 2.4b; 18.5; Rev. 14.18). Treading the winepress is an expression used to demonstrate the Lord's anger (Joel 4.13; Rev. 14.20). Drinking "wine from the cup of God's fury" makes the people of the earth drunk (Is. 63.6; Rev. 14.10).

The mothers of the princes of Israel are compared to vines whose strong rods became rulers' scepters and whose height was exalted above the clouds (Ezek. 19.10-11). Ezekiel spoke of Zedekiah, Judah's last king, whom Nebuchadnezzar installed as the vine planted in the vineyard of Israel (Ezek. 17.5-8). "Have regard for this vine and the stem/reed [kanah] which your right hand has planted, and on the son whom you have made strong for yourself" (Ps. 80.15-16).

Jacob's family swelled in Egypt until it became a mighty nation. It was then uprooted andtransplanted in more productive soil in the land of Canaan: "You pulled out a vine from Egypt. You drove out nations and planted it. You cleared a place for it, and it took deep root and filled the land" (Ps. 80.9). In time, Israel occupied a central place in the world's economy, but due to a multitude of transgressions she became prey for the gentile nations. Those who passed by her "plucked" her fruit (Jer. 12.10-14). To pluck is *arah*, which Raphael Hirsch suggests is a word related to being naked (1997: 81).

According to Margaret Barker, the stem of the vine represented the *Davidic* ruler, King Solomon—a tree that was a great vine (2014: 435). The parable of the trees in Judges (9) lists the olive, the fig, and the vine who would come to reign over the people. Although in context this is a reference to local judges, Nogah Hareuveni states in his book *Tree and Shrub in Our Biblical Heritage* that the olive tree was King David, the fig tree was King Saul, and the grapevine was King Solomon.

King Solomon's reign epitomized the golden age of Israel's united monarchy. As part of his coronation ceremony, Solomon rode down to the Gihon Spring on the king's mule (*peredah* female wild donkey). *Yeshua* later told his disciples to bring him a donkey (*chamor* male) and a colt from a nearby village to ride as he descended from the Mount of Olives into Jerusalem for his own triumphal entry (Matt. 21.1-10). "Behold, your king is coming to you, a righteous one bringing salvation. He is lowly, riding on a donkey—on a colt, the foal of a donkey" (Zech. 9.9).

Yeshua declared himself to be the true vine. He said his disciples were the branches and his Father was the vinedresser (Jn. 15). Why did *Yeshua* choose the imagery of a vine? Was he referring to King Solomon? Was he conveying to them that the restoration of the *Davidic* dynasty was at hand? He said they were bound together and that as his branches they would bear his fruit. According to Barker, there is a chiastic structure within this passage (verses 7-17) with verse eleven being the center: "These things I have spoken to you that my joy may be in you and that your joy may be full." This fullness of joy comes when the *Davidic* king takes his rightful place on the throne and produces good fruit in the vineyard.

King Solomon once planted a vineyard at Baal-Hamon (Song of Songs 8.11) and entrusted it to caretakers. *Yeshua* shared a parable with his disciples about a "man" who planted a vineyard and leased it to tenant farmers while he was away on a journey (Mk. 12.1-9; Luke 20.9-16). The man sent servants to collect the fruit at harvest time, but they were either beaten or killed by the farmers. Finally, he sent his "beloved son" and heir, but he too was killed. In the context of the first century, the vineyard represented the Second Temple, and the tenant farmers were the chief priests and ruling authorities who rejected the Son of the vineyard as the owner. *Yeshua* warned that not one stone of the Temple would be left upon another, and in 70 CE, under the Roman general Titus, the Temple and the city of Jerusalem were captured and destroyed just as *Yeshua* had said.

Isaiah laid bare the heart of *YHWH* when he wrote, "Let me sing of my beloved, a song of my beloved, about His vineyard. My beloved had a vineyard in a very fertile hill. He dug it out and cleared its stones, planted it with a choice vine, built a tower in the midst of it, and even cut out a winepress" (Is. 5.1-2). Isaiah also said the vineyard would be destroyed and given to others to manage: "I will make known to you what I will do to my vineyard: I will take away the hedge, and it will be eaten up. I will break down the fence, and it will be trodden. I will lay it waste: it will not be pruned or hoed but briers and thorns will come up" (Is. 5.5-6).

Isaiah's Song of the Vineyard (Is. 27.2-3) is connected to the Song of Songs which was written by King Solomon. Song of Songs is a love story between Solomon and the House he built for *YHWH*. "Come, my beloved... let us go out early to the vineyards—let us see if the vine has budded, if their blossoms have opened... there I will give you my love" (7.13).

The Temple is the Bride; she is black like the tents of Kedar (the Tabernacle) and beautiful like the curtains of Solomon (in the Temple the veil was scarlet, blue, purple and linen). "The beams of our houses are cedar trees, our panels are cypress trees" (1.17). Solomon's Temple resembled a garden. The cedar on the interior walls of the House were carved with gourds and open flowers. The walls and the doors were engraved with cherubim and palm trees. Capitals on the pillars were shaped like lilies (I Kings 6.18, 29-32, 7.19).

The Song is filled with garden imagery that reminds the reader of Eden's sanctuary where the fullness of creation is joined in intimacy with the creator God. "[The] Song returns us to Eden with the intent of imaginatively healing the ruptures that occurred there: between man and woman, between humanity and God, between human and non-human creation" (Davis, 2003 *Reading the Song Iconographically*).

YHWH's sanctuary is magnified throughout the Song of Songs as a reminder of the long awaited relational and creational restoration. In the Song, final deliverance has come. The exile is over, and humanity is dwelling permanently in His presence. God's people have drawn near to Him in intimate relationship. When that day comes "[e]veryone will sit under his own vine and fig tree, and no one will make them afraid, for the LORD Almighty has spoken" (Micah 4.4).

God's creative purpose is to foster within us a deep love for *YHWH*, for our families, and for our neighbors. Davis summarizes it this way: "the poet of the Song understood that the well-being of our world—not just of the individual person, but of the world as a whole—depends upon the human capacity to cultivate intimacy, indeed, love, in all three relational areas." This is true creational healing and restoration!

Chaos

In the Bible, chaos is synonymous with the destruction of the Temple—the result of covenant breaking. We find chaos manifestingas signs in the heavens tied to language of cosmic upheaval: the sun darkened, the moon did not give its light, the stars fell from heaven (Matt 24). These cosmic disturbances were due to Israel's covenant breaking; they were not the cause of it. Jon Levenson argues that chaos is the key to understanding the reality of suffering in the world. It is a non-personified force that strains against the boundaries God established in the creation of the world. Chaos results when humanity exalts its own moral authority over God's and offers allegiance to other gods. In the ancient world, kings, by their evil actions, could cause the cosmos to collapse which in turn created chaos and upheaval in the societal order.

Creation, on the other hand, is synonymous with temple building. Building a house has multiple meanings in Scripture. "House" might refer to the cosmos, a kingdom, a king's dynasty, a physical temple, a community, or a family.

Regardless of the intended meaning, the consequences are the same: break the covenant; destroy the house. Throughout Scripture, broken covenants result in exile which is a condition associated with barrenness, loss of intimacy and relationship, and separation from the Presence of God: chaos.

Barren women are often a metaphor for the primal state of chaos. Giving birth denotes a reversal of that chaos. We find instances of God sending instruments of judgment, usually the gentile nations, against a house that has become defiled. This judgment leads to exile—a place of thistles, thorns, and briars where things die and nothing grows. Death without subsequent renewal is an anti-creational state. A curse is simply the result of violating God's natural order. The breakdown of societal order can be called a curse for it is the consequence of upending natural law.

The flood story shows the divine struggle between chaos and order within the ANE mythological tradition. The term *Chaoskampf* is often used, and it depicts this struggle as a battle between a local hero/deity and a chaos monster such as a serpent or dragon. Morales explains that *Chaoskampf* is a "motif linked in the Old Testament to moral and/or social disorder so the ultimate purpose of the deluge is to purify" (2012: 129).

In the Exodus story, chaos is depicted as destructive swarms of locusts, frogs, blight, boils, hail, darkness, etc. The Nile River turns to blood, and in a final blow, the firstborn of man and animal are killed. The ten plagues symbolize a return to primeval chaos and judgment for those guilty of enslaving Israel. Pharaoh's responsibility as ruler was to maintain order and stability for his people. His inability to stop God's judgment leaves Egypt immersed in those chaotic forces that show the powerlessness of Pharaoh against YHWH (Fretheim 2010: 106-7).

In the ANE world, raging seas were associated with chaos. They aroused a sense of foreboding for the people and created an environment of instability, unpredictability, and danger. Viewed as the domain of beasts and sea monsters, the sea was a symbol of rebellion against God: "You [Adonai] rule over the swelling of the sea. When its waves mount up, you still them. You crushed Rahab like a slain one. You scattered your enemies with your mighty arm" (Ps. 89.10-11).

In Revelation, the seas represent the dominion of the enemy, which at the time of Revelation's writing would have been the gentile nation of Rome. Daniel (7) depicts four great beasts coming up from the sea. These beasts represent rulers from the gentile nations (Babylon, Persia, Greece, and Rome) who oppressed Israel. The seven-headed beast with ten horns that rose out of the sea was likely Caesar Nero, the fifth Roman emperor (54-68 CE) and the quintessential tyrant most associated with extravagance, debauchery, and persecution. He was a man of extreme cruelty who inflicted unimaginable torture on first-century Christians. Christians were often torn apart by wild dogs, nailed to crosses, and made into human torches to illuminate the city of Rome. Though these persecutions were largely confined to Rome, Nero's mindset set the stage for persecution elsewhere in the empire.

Von Rad describes floods and raging rivers this way: "[it] gushes up throwing yawning chasms onto the earth, then there is a destruction of the entire cosmic system. The two halves of the chaotic primeval sea, separated—one up, the other below—by God's creative government are again united; creation begins to sink again into chaos" (1972: 128). A flood is often compared to hostile warriors in battle attacking and undoing God's creation (Waltke 2001: 140). The Sumerian word for flood is *amaru* and is related to devastating streams of humanity or the destructive power of hostile troops. Invading tribes were called *amurrium* (Lang 2008: 223). Halloway describes this as "the imaginative [equating] of invading hordes penetrating lower Mesopotamia via the Tigris and Euphrates with destructive fluvial floods racing downstream along these life-giving rivers" (1991: 173).

The book of Revelation (9) describes another chaotic force: a locust-like army of "200 thousand, thousand" horsemen (a large formation Roman legion was 10,000 men) with iron breastplates that were fiery red, hyacinth blue, and sulfur yellow. The soldiers are described as having heads like lions, hair like women, and tails like scorpions. Within the context of the time and setting, the scorpion was a Roman ballista—a siege engine that hurled arrows. The Roman equestrian helmet resembled a "crown of gold" with an attached face mask. High ranking officers in the Roman cavalry wore these ornately decorated crowns that were adorned with long hair. This apocalyptic language depicts a five-month siege by the Roman army against Judea that ended on the 9th of Av in 70 CE. Under Apollyon, likely a reference to General Titus, the second Temple was destroyed.

The Bible speaks often of the Day of the Lord as a day filled with cosmic disturbances: violent winds, a darkened sun, a blood moon that fails to give light, and stars that fall from the sky. It is described as a day filled with darkness and gloominess. The prophet Joel described it in graphic terms as a day in which cankerworms and caterpillars devoured all plant life. Devastation of the grain crop led to the loss of the wheat and barley harvest and left storehouses and granaries ruined. Grapevines withered, and the fig, pomegranate, and palm trees all wilted (Joel 1).

This destruction Joel vividly memorialized was the result of Israel's covenant breaking. Sometimes she strayed so far that God's hand of protection was completely removed. Foreign invaders attacked and destroyed fields, vineyards, and orchards. The monarchy was upended, the nation was pillaged, and masses of people were killed or enslaved. Forced into exile, they were stripped naked of their culture and identity and made to live under the thumb of cruel and oppressive tyrants. "[God's] anger will be kindled against you, so He will shut up the sky so that there will be no rain and the soil will not yield its produce. Then you will perish quickly from the good land *Adonai* is giving you" (Deut. 11.16-17).

Human slavery was and is the epitome of societal chaos. The goal of the gods was to turn humans into worker bees for the empire so the elites never knew hunger or lack. Without a doubt, slavery is the most profitable of all enterprises going back millennium. Large swaths of mankind living as serfs under brutal and vicious regimes has been the historical norm.

Slavery was an integral part of ancient Rome's social order. Nearly forty percent of Rome's population was made up of enslaved people—many of them prisoners of war who were bought and sold as property in the slave markets.Slaves were forced into tenement housing where they endured overcrowding and life-threatening conditions. Constant fear of fire, collapse, and flooding from the Tiber River were a daily reality. Roman streets were very dangerous places. Prisoners were often bound with ropes, sewn into heavy sacks (with a snake or two thrown in for good measure), and tossed into the river. Christians were persecuted in especially brutal ways under Caesar Nero (64 BCE). Like in many ancient cultures, Rome's ruling elites were cruel and bloodthirsty, willing to torture and put to death anyone without hesitation.

It was into this world that *Yeshua* came. Surrounded by this hostile environment, *Yeshua* confronted the power structures of the day and railed against the chaos they produced. But he did not do this in the way most expected. He responded differently by encouraging the Jewish people to see another way. He reminded Israel of the heartbeat of the Torah: ethical justice and morality which is the glue that holds societies together. He taught in parables, he used apocalyptic language to protest and resist world power, and he advanced kingdom principles such as forgiveness, self-denial, love, humility and service. He taught the essence of *YHWH's* kingdom which was and is creational order that leads to life and freedom and extolls the intrinsic value, worth, and dignity of every individual.

As In The Days of Noah

"For just as the days of Noah were, so will be the coming of the Son of Man. For in those days before the flood, they were eating and drinking, marrying and giving in marriage until the day Noah entered the ark. And they did not understand until the flood came and swept them all away. So shall it be at the coming of the Son of Man" (Matt. 24. 37-39; Luke 17.25-26).

The Olivet Discourse, as this is often called, contains language related to the Temple and the priesthood. It outlines the consequences for the nation that breaks covenant with *YHWH*. The geo-political backdrop of the chapter includes Rome, the Herodian dynasty, and the Temple's ruling authorities.

Prophecy buffs have long debated the meaning of these verses. When seeking an interpretation, it is helpful to remember that the New Testament writers often chose to draw parallels to characters from the Hebrew Bible and extra-biblical literature (most notably Moses, Elijah, and *Enoch* in the book of Jude) to make a theological point, not a historical one. The writer of Matthew was purposely placing Noah in a first century setting to address the coming destruction and to remind the reader that, like He did in saving Noah and his family, *YHWH* will preserve righteous seed.

The Olivet Discourse is filled with references to a cataclysmic upheaval of the powers of heaven along with natural disasters, persecutions, wars, and violent insurrection. The message to the elect was to flee the coming disaster and the ferocious assault the Roman army was about to inflict on the nation. His people would find rest and safety by entering His Presence in the "ark of Noah."

Rome's response to the Jewish Revolt (66-70CE) was to crush all resistance. The Temple was destroyed for the second time in history, and the Jews were scattered once again. They would live outside the Promised Land without a temple and without a king. Judaism did manage to flourish by transforming its cultic life in the Temple to the synagogue, the family Sabbath table, and the prayer services as a substitute for the ritual offerings. In this, the Jews stayed tied to their ancient traditions even though their national identity was lost.

At the same time, first century Christians, believers in Messiah, saw the destruction of the Temple and the monarchy as the end of an era and the dawn of a new age with the faith of Abraham as its foundation. This required a reshaping of the ancient traditions. This was not a new religion though, nor was it a replacement for the "old" as some Christians believe. It was not a new way. Rather, it was simply a response to the upheaval of having lost temple, priesthood, and king.

The destruction of the city and Temple simulated the chaos at creation when the world was *tohu v'vohu*: empty and without form. In the beginning, out of the chaos and disorder, God raised up a man, Adam, as His representative king, to serve and to work the garden and to mediate between God and mankind. He did the same for Noah after the flood when Noah built a vineyard. In the same way, God resurrected *Yeshua* the Messiah, the anointed one, to inaugurate a new creation temple and to complete the Genesis blueprint. As the dark powers converged on the tree, *Yeshua* nullified the abuse that the ruling elites of the world along with their evil gods had unleashed upon the people. Healing, deliverance, freedom, stability, and order would now fill a world that was consistently immersed in chaos.

The Olivet Discourse begins with *Yeshua* "going away" from the Temple and taking his disciples up on the Mount of Olives. There, he points out the Temple buildings from across the Kidron valley and declares that not one stone will be left upon another. *Yeshua's* disciples then ask for the sign of his "coming" and the end of the age. "Coming" is the English translation of the Greek word *parousia*. A more accurate translation, however, would be "coming presence." Anciently, a king's presence was connected to his enthronement. At the conclusion of the coronation ceremony, the king took his seat on his throne and began to rule. Were the disciples asking for the sign of *Yeshua's* enthronement and the inauguration of his kingdom? "Lord, are you restoring the kingdom to Israel at this time" (Acts 1.6)? Were they really asking the most important question of all: if the Temple is destroyed, where will the Divine Presence rest? These questions are answered throughout the book of Acts as the Exodus story is retold from the perspective of a new creation people.

Acts begins with *Yeshua* and his disciples again on the Mount of Olives (1.12). He commands his disciples to remain in Jerusalem and to wait for the promise of the Father—the immersion in the *Ruach HaKodesh*, the Holy Spirit, the Divine Presence. The Spirit would empower them to become living "martyrs" (in the Greek) as they went out from Jerusalem to the ends of the earth. (The Hebrew word for martyrs or witnesses is *eduth* and refers to legal testimonies.) "After saying all this—while they were watching—He was taken up, and a cloud received Him out of their sight" (Acts 1.9). *Yeshua* was taken up in a cloud on the Mount of Olives in the same way Moses went up in a cloud on Mount Sinai (Ex. 24.15).

The transfiguration in Matthew (17.1-3) is similar to the event mentioned in Acts (1). In both narratives, two men, Moses and Elijah in Matthew and unnamed men in Acts, are standing in white clothing talking with or standing near *Yeshua*. These men were not the actual historical characters, but history was drawn upon by the writer to make a point: *Yeshua's* exodus (resurrection) is Israel's exodus. *Yeshua's* deliverance from death is Israel's deliverance from death. Appearing in glory, these figures were speaking of *Yeshua's* departure, that is, his Exodus (Luke 9.31 in the Greek), which was about to take place in Jerusalem.

The sign of the "end of the age" meant the end of the old order! No longer would the Temple's ruling authorities subjugate the people, especially through debt. Israel's jubilee was coming which meant freedom for slaves, freedom from debt, and a return of the land to its original owners. The end of the age never meant the end of the world but rather a release from the powers that abused the people and made them captive to sin and death. The destruction of the corrupted Temple was the sign of *Yeshua's* vindication.

In the ANE world, a temple stood as a bulwark against the waters of chaos; *Yeshua* prophesied the destruction of the Temple because of its deeply-rooted corruption (particularly by the high priest Annas and his family) that created chaos in the land instead of guarding against it. John wrote in his Gospel that *Yeshua* dumped out the coins of the money-changers and overturned their tables. He did so declaring that zeal for his Father's House had consumed him. When the Judean leaders asked for a sign, he responded, "Destroy this Temple and in three days I will raise it up" (Jn. 2.19-22). The leaders, knowing it took the Herodians forty-six years to build the Temple, chided him. But *Yeshua*, of course, was speaking of his body as the new creation Temple! *Yeshua* became the real threat to the current powers—a threat that would get him killed.

Before the flood, in Noah's day, people were eating and drinking and marrying and giving in marriage. This oft-quoted line is likely speaking of priestly functions rather than everyday life. In fact, priests were unable to perform their ritual duties in the Temple unless they were married. Eating and drinking were ritual, ceremonial acts in the Temple; eating meat and bread and drinking wine were part of the daily service. If priest/kings in Noah's day were performing their daily duties up until the time of the flood perhaps the flood was judgment for their corruption.

According to Matthew (24), the people didn't understand until the flood (armies) came and swept them all away. Two men were in the field. Two women were grinding at the mill. One was taken and one was left (Matt. 24.37-41). New Testament scholar N.T. Wright suggests this is related to exile—a reminder of the Babylonian exile when some were left behind. Were the days of Noah likened to exile? Noah is the first "left behind" one, a *sha'ar*, or remnant (Gen. 7.23). The remnant is the one who will remain in Israel to rebuild God's House. The one taken is taken into exile.

Is Matthew (24) also speaking of the return of the Divine Presence to a new creation temple? Many of the parables speak of a master or king who returns from a journey. Wright suggests these parables are speaking of the Divine Presence returning to Jerusalem and not necessarily of *Yeshua* returning to the earth.

The Mount of Olives was also called the Mount of *Maschiach* (messiah) or the Mount of Anointment. On it thrived groves of olive trees that produced oil to anoint Israel's kings. Oil became symbolic for the Divine Presence, the Holy Spirit. Another special ceremony took place near the summit of the mount. To mark the start of each new month, signal fires were lit confirming the new moon had been sighted.

Yeshua and his disciples sat on the Mount of Olives near an ancient altar close to the summit. On this altar, the offering of the red heifer was completely consumed. The ashes were mixed with spring water and used to purify those who had become ritually impure through contact with the dead. An immersion bath, also located at the altar, was specifically for the high priest if he chose to perform the ritual for purification (Dye 2018: 128).

Yeshua commanded his students to go and make disciples of all nations (Matt. 28.18-20). How would they respond? It was not possible to become ritually pure outside the land of Israel. If the Temple was destroyed, ritual purification for corpse uncleanness would become impossible. Did they understand that they were being equipped with the Divine Presence to elevate the world from death? Did they understand that the Divine Presence within them meant the world could no longer contaminate them?Paul reminds us that the body is a temple of the *Ruach HaKodesh*, the Holy Spirit, the Divine Presence that was bought with a price.

Shortly following the Olivet Discourse, in the evening of *Chag haMatzah* or the Feast of Unleavened Bread, *Yeshua* and his disciples partook of the Passover seder. At the close of the meal, *Yeshua* said, " 'I will not drink of this fruit of the vine from now on until that day when I drink it new with you in My Father's kingdom.' And when they had sung a hymn, they went out to the Mount of Olives" (Matt. 26.29-30 NKJV). The hymn they sang was likely Psalm 136, the Great Hallel, chanted in Temple times as the Passover lambs were slain. It was recited during the last cup of wine which was called the cup of redemption—a reminder of *YHWH's* redemption from bondage in Egypt.

When would *Yeshua* drink the last cup with them in his Father's kingdom? Was this fulfilled as he hung on the tree, tasted the sour wine, and declared "It is finished" (Jn. 19.30)? The Lamb of God was now slain and would soon be resurrected. And so began the great creational reset as a new creation temple/community was born.

Psalm 136 is a responsive psalm in which each verse concludes with *Ki l'olam chasdo*, "His mercy endures forever!" The psalm celebrates *YHWH's* conquering of the sea for His people. It is a declaration that He alone has done great wonders: He made the heavens by His wisdom, He spread the earth on the waters, He made the sun to illuminate the day and the moon to illuminate the night, He led Israel out of Egypt with a strong hand and outstretched arm, He cut the sea into parts, He drowned pharaoh in the deep, and He struck down mighty kings. The psalm is a declaration of *YHWH's* universal rule over nature throughout history, with mankind owing its sustenance to His sovereignty. He is the One true God among all the gods, highest above all other powers. He is active in daily life and is the foundation of ordered society.

Cultural Chaos

> The tyrant, who in order to hold his power, suppresses every superiority, does away with good men, forbids education and light, controls every movement of the citizens and, keeping them under a perpetual servitude, wants them to grow accustomed to baseness and cowardice, has his spies everywhere to listen to what is said in the meetings, and spreads dissension and calumny among the citizens and impoverishes them, is obliged to make war in order to keep his subjects occupied and impose on them the permanent need of a chief.
>
> ARISTOTLE (384-322 BCE)

Aristotle brilliantly summarized the default position of the world's tyrants. Today's globalist elites are repeating the same pattern laid out so many millennia ago. Civilization again finds itself under a powerful spell that has seized the minds of humanity. We are on the precipice of self-destruction.

America's Founding Fathers understood tyranny well; they designed our Constitutional Republic to protect us from the iron grip of totalitarianism. They understood, however, that only a people of faith and virtue would be able to prevent humanity's eventual descent into chaos and anarchy. John Adams recognized that America's constitution was made for a "moral and religious people" and was "wholly inadequate to the government of any other." As Samuel Adams once said, "Neither the wisest constitution nor the wisest laws will secure the liberty and happiness of a people whose manners are universally corrupt." Unfortunately, America has left behind "good manners" to become socially, spiritually, and ethically bankrupt.

We have abandoned the noblest of all virtues: personal responsibility that leads to true freedom. Lawlessness has become our guiding creed. The book of Judges warns us from history, "[in] those days there was no king. Everyone did what was right in his own eyes" (21.25). As a nation, we have abandoned the lessons from our past and have strayed from once common values. We have abdicated our Judeo-Christian roots in virtually every area of life: government, business, law, medicine, education, entertainment, military, and religion. Patriots watch in disbelief as our most cherished institutions crumble under the weight of a new religion imposed forcefully by the minority: a collectively "woke," cancel culture. Americans who resist the latest cultural indoctrination are treated as heretics who must be publicly shamed and humiliated, unpersoned, or permanently destroyed. We are in a moral free fall; where we will bottom out is anyone's guess.

Feelings and subjective thought rule the day to become the gold standard of the new religion. Objective truth, standards of right and wrong, rational thinking, and reasoned debate have all but been erased. Though adherence to Judeo-Christian values and ethics will protect us from societal chaos, we have rejected these values and our moral foundation has been reduced to rubble. Biblical illiteracy in modern America has contributed to our decline as a nation.

America has been fundamentally transformed into a Marxist, dystopian nightmare and is being governed by a variety of woke creeds: social justice, liberation theology, equity, (diversity and inclusion), critical race theory, and militant transgenderism. The totalitarian Left has replaced class warfare with race warfare to further divide the nation and cause the fabric of society to finally unravel.

Amidst all this distraction, America has turned a blind eye to the greatest blight of all, the human/sex trafficking and organ harvesting trade. This alone will define us as a faithless, soulless, materialistic, godless culture! Additionally, the ruling class has looted America for decades, passing the nation's proceeds on to the Chinese Communist Party all in an effort to hide the coming economic destruction of America. The nation has also been systemically corporatized, which has led to the decimation of small businesses, the healthcare system, and the legal profession just for starters.

Today, we are drowning in information but starving for wisdom. Many of our leaders in government and business are fools who say in their heart, "'There is no God.' They are corrupt; their deeds are vile; there is no one who does good" (Ps. 14.1). They reject God and do not fear Him. As a result, they lack the wisdom and common sense necessary for righteous governing. The policies they adopt often reflect mental, moral, and ethical failure.

Throughout history, the elites have continually supported the eradication of the nuclear family: a God-ordained institution that serves as the bulwark against cultural tyranny, government overreach, and the excesses of immoral behavior. Aristotle once wrote, "The family is the basic cell of all human society, the primary association of human beings..." He concluded that the family "represents nature in its clearest manifestation." Today our families, our houses of worship, and our once bustling civic organizations have all eroded to such a degree that we've lost the glue that holds our communities together.

Nearly 100 years ago, G.K. Chesterton noted that the family was the check on state power and that weakening the family would defeat freedom itself. For modern society, the family as an institution has lost and continues to lose its social significance. Over the last sixty years, the administrative state's welfare policies have systematically destroyed the family by scorning the institution of marriage, advancing deviant sexual behavior, advocating divorce, supporting abortion, and encouraging fatherlessness. Through its godless policies, the state has contributed mightily to the destruction of the most important element of all functioning societies.

The beautiful distinctions between men and women are now scorned. Manhood is under near constant assault—likely contributing to the rise of transgenderism. Complaints about "toxic masculinity" have reached a frenzy. The modern answer to the age-old problem of abusive men is simply to rid the world of the strong, competent ones. This mental assault has resulted in men becoming lazy, weak, and cowardly (speaking in general terms, of course) and has produced men who put up little resistance when crisis comes. They often fail at their most fundamental calling: to protect and defend the family at all cost.

By contrast, modern society has elevated women to goddess-like status. Long past shattering the glass ceiling in the workplace, today's feminist movement pushes women to completely replace men in their societal roles. Camille Paglia equates the rise of feminism with the collapse of Western civilization. She says feminism is often based on denigrating men. Feminism defines women as the oppressed and men as oppressors, and as a result it trivializes every good thing that individual men do. She suggests ancient history must be taught in schools to show how men, over the centuries, have given their lives, their labor, and their love in support of women and children.

Gender confusion has taken hold of our young people and is being actively pushed throughout the public education system. Society is positioned on a dangerous, slippery slope when the culture no longer recognizes the innate biological differences between men and women, and places roadblocks in the way of the perpetuation of civilization. Identity, once viewed through the lens of society as a whole, was highly valued in ancient cultures. Today, identity has been perverted to discard society's needs and focus on the selfishly individual thoughts and wants of each person. This is realized in the Left's narrow political agenda aimed solely at gender, sexual orientation, and ethnicity.

The church has also been taken hostage by the dark forces of cultural chaos. Questionable sociological, psychological, and political agendas have seeped into many mainline congregations. In some quarters, the church is nothing more than an advocate for social justice, an apologist for BLM and Antifa, and a cheerleader for the militant LGBQT+ and their agenda. American pastors have, more often than not, failed to speak out against these destructive societal trends. Some churches happily advance cultural chaos so as not to lose congregants, weekly tithes and offerings, or their highly exalted 501C3 tax exempt status.

In many cases, the church, which is the most essential institution in the community, was first to bow at the altar of fear when the virus hit. The cowardice shown by many leaders in surrendering to the tyranny of the state is abhorrent. Many remained silent, never pushed back against unconstitutional orders, and kept their doors closed. Instead of meeting the needs of a community in crisis, they abdicated their chief responsibility and chose to worship at the altar of "safety."

Nothing says chaos like the culture's embrace of trans-genderism, scientism, and trans-humanism—the latest iterations of modern America's (and the world's) fastest growing religion: technocracy. One wonders how anything could be more destructive to civil and societal order.

Transgenderism is creating societal chaos by normalizing gender confusion instead of addressing the root cause which is mental illness. The propaganda arm continually promotes dangerous therapies such as puberty blockers and surgery to the very young. These harmful treatments can affect brain development and cause other problems that result when puberty is unnaturally delayed. This is the latest effort from the left in the culture war to indoctrinate our children. Though it appears to be a "fad," transgenderism abuses troubled kids and forces life-altering medical procedures that will permanently destroy their lives. Many victims are deeply troubled, and an unsettling number have resorted to suicide as a result of going without proper treatment. Those struggling need real, life-changing help from families, the church, the community, or para ministries dedicated to the issue.

Scientism is another example of the new religion of technocracy. At its core are questionable scientific interpretations based on dubious methods of investigation. Originally, the term was coined by Friedrich Hayek who defined scientism as a "slavish imitation of the method and language of science." Traditional scientific methods and practices have been held hostage which has allowed scientism's gatekeepers to push their social, political, and medical agendas. Today, the purveyors of scientism have rarely shown the true science, data, or evidence surrounding COVID; and worse, they have purposely misinterpreted what facts they have shown.

Scientific data has been buried, manipulated or censored in order to allow for unscientific lockdowns of the economy and the greatest transfer of wealth in human history from the middle class to the oligarchs. Lee Smith, in his article *The Thirty Tyrants* (Feb. 3, 2021), said, "There is a good reason why lockdowns—quarantining those who are not sick—had never been previously employed as a public health measure. The leading members of a city, state, or nation do not imprison its own unless they mean to signal that they are imposing collective punishment on the population at large. It had never been used before as a public health measure because it is a widely recognized instrument of political repression."

Trans-humanism is a metaphysical belief system that asserts immortality can be achieved if advanced science is applied to the human condition. The advocates of trans-humanism see the "blessings" of human evolution through the eyes of new technologies like AI (artificial intelligence). Its goal is to eliminate aging and enhance man's intellectual abilities. Trans-humanism advocates say technology can overcome human limitations to move us "beyond human" through things like chip design, robotics, and AI. For the technocratic gods, death is merely a disease that can be conquered—just a technical problem to be addressed through engineering. Trans-humanism will likely mean the end of humanity as we know it.

Julian Huxley (1887-1975), known as the father of trans-humanism, was an English evolutionary biologist and eugenicist. He believed advancements in technology would enhance the human condition. While serving as Director General of UNESCO, he advocated for population control, planting seeds that have borne fruit among today's globalist elites.

For Huxley, religious belief needed to be reformed because it inhibited man's evolutionary drive. He believed secularism would ultimately replace Christianity as a religion because knowledge and relationship with self was more important than knowledge and relationship with God. Huxley understood Christianity's worldwide spread had come about through long periods of deliberation and through passionate expression that allowed human creativity to be released and shape the entire western world.

Trans-humanism is the pursuit of immortality—the last frontier in technological advancement. Today's tech oligarchs have attained immeasurable power, god-like influence, and untold resources; they now desire eternal life which they believe can be achieved through advanced technology. Of course, there is nothing new under the sun. Like the kings of old, the globalist elites and Silicon Valley oligarchs have become obsessed with living forever.

According to Gab's Andrew Torba, members of the globalist cabal want to become among the first human beings to "transcend" beyond the limitations of human biology to become as gods. "You are gods, and you are all sons of Elyon, yet you will die like men, and will fall like any of the princes" (Ps. 82.6-7). They believe enhanced man will be eternal man. Technocracy's rallying cry is to produce a race of men superior in quality to any ever known on Earth. Eugenics is their solution.

The social critic Christopher Lasch explains in his 1979 book, *The Culture of Narcissism*, that fear of death has taken on a new intensity and in the process has deprived society of the values of religion and posterity. He says dread of old age is part of the cult of self. The goal is entering a technological utopia without being subjected to old age. Transhumanists are attempting to manufacture eternal life without God.

A strong faith in God and a recognition of His perfect judgment in the afterlife form a protective hedge against the fear of death. John Zmirak explains that if you lose the idea of an afterlife in which you are accountable for your actions in this life, then you lose the basis of liberty. America's Founders understood this. They knew a Constitutional Republic functioned only for a people who believed their actions affected the life to come. Zmirak adds that, [in] such a system, churches are free, families are free, citizens are free. They're free to thrive, to fail, to sink or swim, to face the burden of choice and the consequences of failure" (Zmirak, *To Elites, We are*

Mystery Meatballs. Nothing More, The Stream online August 6, 21). Without a belief in an afterlife, society will show no concern or care for the generations that follow. With a belief in an afterlife, people will take risks and willingly endure pain and suffering to leave behind a lasting legacy that future generations may build upon.

All of this paints a rather bleak picture of not just the current reality in America but the condition of humanity as a whole. The world is clearly in crisis. America is clearly a nation in crisis. Our dilapidated infrastructure is the perfect metaphor for the soul of our nation. Add to that a dysfunctional healthcare system, a massive spike in violent crime, the spread of homeless encampments, an opioid crisis (leaving our cities rife with crime and sidewalks full of needles, feces, and garbage), and an all-out invasion of illegal immigrants (many with covid and other diseases) freely crossing our southern border. With each passing day, America looks more and more like Venezuela or Cuba. Restoring sanity to the nation means we will have to rebuild our broken down house!

On the political front, restoring our Republic is key.It will be incumbent upon every patriot to get involved in their government in some way, either running for office or helping someone else run. The country will be restored one precinct at a time, one school board at a time, and one town council at a time—the focus needs to be on our local communities first and foremost.

There are some encouraging signs. We are seeing the first glimmer of hope in the political arena: mama bears are rising up at school board meetings to rescue their children from rabid, Marxist indoctrination. Veterans who are battle-tested are seeking public office in many states. A movement of "little guys," known as the Ape Army, is pushing back against Wall Street's predatory practices by buying and holding American stocks. All over the country, patriots are waking up to the reality that our country has been hijacked by the globalist elites, most of whom are inside our own government.

A cultural secession will likely be necessary to preserve the next generation. Jacob's clan went down to Egypt where they flourished inside another nation for four hundred years. Egypt's disdain for the nomadic family resulted in their being apportioned prime grazing land in Goshen (Gen. 46.33-34). In time, the tribes were severely persecuted and oppressed by the Egyptians until *YHWH* birthed them through the sea to become an independent, free nation.

We need to embrace the traditions that held this nation together and focus again on what will sustain us as one nation under God. The Pilgrims showed us the way; they began their journey to America by first renewing a covenant with the Almighty. Then they went to work building a country. We will need to invest blood, sweat, and tears in our local communities. We will need to hold on to truth and faith, putting righteousness and true biblical justice ahead of our own comforts or even needs.

Nothing in history is inevitable as our future; we can change our course as we learn from the past. Tyrannical ideologies lack the capacity for permanence. Evil simply cannot be sustained forever.

Any hope for a long-term solution will require the healing of America's soul. As the global juggernaut devours freedom everywhere it finds it still breathing, Americans have been forced to re-evaluate their lives and consider what, and in whom, they believe. We must return to our Judeo-Christian roots and restore our moral and ethical foundations if we have any hope of societal order. All will rest, however, with God's covenant people who choose to walk as a beacon of light in a very dark world. It will be a difficult road both for those who choose to walk it and for those who are caught unaware, and in many cases it will be a life-threatening one.

Creational Order

"For the creation eagerly awaits the revelation of the sons of God... For we know that the whole creation groans together and suffers birth pains until now—and not only creation, but even ourselves. We ourselves who have the firstfruits of the Spirit, groan inwardly as we eagerly wait for adoption—the redemption of our body" (Rom. 8.19-23).

Creation is the context for *YHWH's* imperial rule! His kingship is rooted in creation; His victory over the waters of chaos established a stable and secure world. *YHWH's* creation set the cosmos free from the tyranny of the gods/rulers of the ancient world and will do the same for us today. Enemy kings and hostile peoples were identified with those primeval waters, but God's throne subdued the waters of chaos (Ps. 29.10).When *Yeshua* walked on the waters, he was representing God's sovereignty in overcoming the nations (Matt. 14.25-26).

Every new beginning is a liberation from crisis. The Genesis creation account is the quintessential story of deliverance and birth through water. God brought forth order and life from a world that was empty and void and in a perpetual state of chaos. Creational order sets people free and liberates them for living an overcoming life. Creation conquers the destructive forces. It restores humanity to its divine image-bearer status.

The pillars of an ordered world are righteousness and justice.When rulers reject these ideals, the wicked prosper and human society suffers. Reality itself is threatened. An ancient king's primary role was to deliver the poor and downtrodden from powerful oppressors.Injustice causes creation to suffer returning humanity to a state of primeval chaos. A king who maintains justice and righteousness, however, allows all God's living creatures to thrive. Nothing has changed.Order is maintained through righteousness and justice both then and now!

Creation theology is infused throughout the Bible and represents a radically different view of human life than the one presented by the world. Creation is synonymous with house/temple building; it is the formation of a covenant between two parties in which life is produced in the image and likeness of God. House building creates order in the universe. Order is synonymous with true liberty, equality, and justice that come from a covenantal relationship with the One True God.

The Bible tells the story of how order is restored from chaos and how good conquers evil in defeating the world's dark powers. We are in a cosmic battle for the rulership of the earth as two kingdoms in conflict are vying for the hearts and souls of men. Evil is countered when it is replaced with acts of creation. Humans were created to join with God in opposing evil and to rescue creation from the kingdom of darkness. This is accomplished through the hand of divine providence accompanied by human agency.

Yeshua's resurrection was the ultimate act of new creation. The gods that enslaved the world were overthrown. Though their earthly lives would continue to be marked by persecution, his people were no longer at the mercy of the ruling elites of the Roman empire. On the cross, a new creation temple was inaugurated in the body of *Yeshua* the Messiah. He came to destroy the works of the evil one and to rebuild a temple/kingdom for the living God. For our part, acts of allegiance to the King of Kings push back the chaos and restore order. "For we know that if the tent, our earthly home, is torn down, we have a building from God—a home not made with human hands, eternal in the heavens. For in this we groan, longing to be clothed with our heavenly dwelling—if indeed, after we have put it on, we will not be found naked" (2 Cor. 5.1-3).

Yeshua launched a radically different kingdom founded on the unthinkable principles of self-giving and self-denial. It was radical for its message of love, humility, and transformation. *Yeshua* challenged his followers to feed his flock if they loved him. He asked them (and asks us) to feed the hungry, to meet the needs of the poor, and to rescue those held captive. The evidence that the Kingdom of Heaven lived in His disciples was confirmed by the good fruit they bore. "I am the vine; you are the branches. The one who abides in Me, and I in him, bears much fruit; for apart from Me, you can do nothing" (Jn 15.5).

We are called to be fruitful and multiply and expand His kingdom through self-sacrifice and selfless love. Love is synonymous with loyalty which is the basis for a covenant relationship. Love is the antidote for evil. Love functions subversively against world power. How do we expand the kingdom and restore order? We act! We serve one another by defending the cause of the widow and the orphan, speaking for the voiceless, holding up the weak and vulnerable, and relieving the suffering of those in distress.

We must ask the Lord our God to equip us for the task ahead and to work in us so that we are prepared to lay down our lives for those in need! We must commit to making life better for those in our sphere of influence. We must ask for the clarity, vision, understanding, and insight to know what to do, when to do it, what to say, and how to say it! Through His love and power, may our service restore order from all the world's chaos.

"Therefore, if anyone is in Messiah, he is a new creation. The old things have passed away; behold, all things have become new" (2 Cor. 5.17).

BIBLIOGRAPHY

Anderson, Bernhard W. (2005) *Creation Versus Chaos*, Eugene, OR: WIPF & Stock.

Apocrypha and Pseudepigrapha of the Old Testament (2004), 2 vols, ed., R.H. Charles, Berkeley: Apocryphile Press.

Averback, Richard (2004) *Ancient Near Eastern Mythography and the Bible*, Academia EDU online article.

Bailey, Lloyd R. (1968) *Israelite 'El Sadday' and Amorite Bel Sade*, Journal of Biblical Literature, 87 (434-438).

Barker, M. (2000) *The Revelation of Jesus Christ*, Edinburgh: T&T Clark.

_____ (2008) *The Gate of Heaven: The History and Symbolism of the Temple in Jerusalem*, Sheffield, England: Phoenix Press.

_____ (2010) *Creation: A Biblical Vision for the Environment*, London: T&T Clark.

Bell, Rob (2019) *What is the Bible?*, San Francisco: Harper One.

Beale, G.K. (2004) *The Temple and the Church's Mission: A Biblical Theology of the Dwelling Place of God*, Downers Grove, IL: Inter Varsity Press.

_____ (2008) *We Become What We Worship: A Biblical Theology of Idolatry*, Downers Grove, IL: Inter Varsity Press.

Blenkinsopp, Joseph (2011) *Creation, Un-Creation, Re-Creation: A Discursive Commentary on Genesis 1-11*, NYC: T & T Clark.

Bodner, Keith (2016) *An Ark on the Nile: The Beginning of the Book of Exodus*, Oxford: Oxford University Press.

Bradshaw, Jeffrey M. (2014) *The Ark and the Tent Temple Symbolism in the story of Noah in Temple Insights: Proceedings of the Interpreter Matthew B. Brown Memorial Conference, The Temple on Mount Zion, 22 September 2012*, ed., William J. Hamblin and David Rolph Seely, Orem, UT: The Interpreter Foundation; Salt Lake City: Eborn Books, (25–66).

Brueggemann, Walter (1997) *Theology of the OT: Testimony, Dispute, Advocacy*, Minneapolis: Fortress Press.

Cassuto, Umberto (1961) *A Commentary on the Book of Genesis: Part III From Noah to Abraham*, trans., I. Abrahams, Jerusalem: Magnes Press.

_____ (1967) *A Commentary on the Book of Exodus*, Jerusalem: Magnes Press.

Childs, Brevard S. (2009) *Myth and Reality in the Old Testament*, Eugene, OR: Wipf & Stock, 2009.

_____ (1965) *The Birth of Moses*, JBL 84 (109-122).

Clements, R.E. (2016) *God and Temple: The Presence of God in Israel's Worship*, Eugene, OR: Wipf & Stock.

Clifford, Richard J. (1972) *The Cosmic Mountain in Canaan and the Old Testament*, HSM

_____ (1984) The Temple and the Holy Mountain, The Temple in Antiquity, ed., T.G. Madsen, Provo, UT: BYU, (107-24).

Cohen, Shaye J.D. (2014) *From the Maccabees to the Mishnah*, Louisville, KY: Westminster John Knox Press.

Coote, Robert B. & Ord, David Robert (2018) *The Bible's First History: From Eden to the Court of David with the Yahwist*, Eugene OR: Wipf and Stock.

Coppens, Phillip (2004) *The Canopus Revelation: Stargate of the Gods and the Ark of Osiris*, Netherlands: Frontier Publishing.

Commentary on the New Testament Use of the Old Testament (2007) eds., G.K. Beale and D.A. Carson, Grand Rapids: Baker Books.

Crenshaw, James L. (1976) *Studies in Ancient Israelite Wisdom*, NYC: KTAV.

Crawford, Cory D (2013) *Noah's Architecture: The Role of Sacred Space in Ancient Near Eastern*

Flood Myths, Constructions of Space IV: Further Developments in Examining Ancient Israel's Social Space, Ed., Mark K. George, London: Bloomsbury/T&T Clark.

Cultural Backgrounds Study Bible (2016) Grand Rapids: Zondervan.

Currid, John (1997) *Ancient Egypt and the Old Testament*, Ada, MI: Baker Publishing Group.

Dalley, Stephanie (1991) *Myths from Mesopotamia: Creation, the Flood, Gilgamesh and others*, Oxford: Oxford University Press.

David, Gary A. (2017) *The Sacred Meaning of the Reed: From Houses and Boats to Rituals, Ceremonies and Portals*, www.theorionzone.com

Davis, Ellen (2003) *Reading the Song Iconographically*, The Journal of Scriptural Reasoning, Durham, NC: Duke University Divinity School.

Davila, James R. (1995) *The Flood Hero as King and Priest*, Journal of Near Eastern Studies, 54 No. 3 July (199-214).

Dozeman, Thomas (2009) *Exodus*, ECC Grand Rapids: Eerdmans.

Dye, Dinah (2016) *The Temple Revealed in Creation: A Portrait of the Family*, Lexington, KY: Foundations in Torah.

_____ (2018) *The Temple Revealed in the Garden: Priests and Kings*, Lexington, KY: Foundations in Torah.

Enns, Pete (2012) *When was Genesis Written and Why Does it Matter*, Biologos Foundation, online article March.

_____ (2019) *How the Bible Actually Works*, San Francisco: HarperOne.

Exile: A conversation with N.T. Wright (2017), *Yet the Sun Will Rise Again*, ed., James M. Scott, Downers Grove, IL: IVP Academic.

Faulconer, James E. (1999) *Scripture Study: Tools and Suggestions*. Provo, UT: Foundation for Ancient Research and Mormon Studies, BYU.

_____ (2007) *Response to Professor Dorrien* ed., Musser and Paulsen Macon, GA: Mercer University Press.

Fishbane (1979) *Text and Texture: Close Readings of Selected Biblical Texts*, NYC.

_____ (1985) *Biblical Interpretation in Ancient Israel*, Oxford: Oxford University Press.

_____ (1998) *Biblical Text and Texture: A Literary Reading of Selected Texts*, Rockport, MA: One World.

Friedland, Roger & Hecht, Richard (1998) *The Bodies of Nations: A Comparative Study of Religious Violence in Jerusalem and Ayodhya*, History of Religions 38, no. 2 Nov.

Fretheim, Terence E. (1996) *Because the Whole Earth is Mine: Theme and Narrative in Exodus*, Interpretation 50.3 (229-239).

_____ (2005) *God and World in the Old Testament: A Relational Theology of Creation*, Nashville, TN: Abingdon Press.

_____ (2010) *Interpretation: Exodus*, Louisville, KY: John Knox Press.

Gage, W.A. (2001) *The Gospel of Genesis: Studies in Protology and Eschatology*, Eugene, OR: Wipf & Stock.

Galenieks, Eriks (2005) *The Nature, Function, and Purpose of the Term She'ol in the Torah, Prophets and Writings*, PhD. Diss., Berrien, MI: Andrews University Seventh-Day Adventist Theological Seminary.

George, Arthur & George, Elena (2014) *The Mythology of Eden*, Lanham, MD: Hamilton bks.

Godawa, Brian (2015) *Leviathan: Sea Dragon of Chaos*, https://godawa.com.

Green, Peter (2012) *Noah's Vineyard: Its narrative Significance and New Creation*

Trajectory, Atlanta: Society of Biblical Literature, March.

Hareuveni, Nogah (1989) *Tree and Shrub in Our Biblical Heritage*, Kiryat Ono, Israel: Neot Kedumim Ltd.

Haupt, Paul (1927) *The Ship of the Babylonian Noah*, BASS 10.

Heaven on Earth (2004) ed., Desmond T. Alexander & Simon Gathercole, *God's Image, His Cosmic Temple, and the High Priest: Towards an Historical and Theological*

Account of the Incarnation, Crispin H.T. Fletcher-Louis, Waynesboro, GA: Paternoster.

Holloway, Steven W. (1991) *What Ship Goes There? The Flood Narratives in the Gilgamesh Epic and Genesis considered in Light of ANE Temple Ideology*, ZAW 103 (328-354).

Homan, Michael M. (2000) *The Divine Warrior in His Tent: A Military Model for Yahweh's Tabernacle*, Bible Review 16:6, December.

Horowitz, David (2018) *Dark Agenda: The War to Destroy Christian America*, West Palm Beach, FL: Humanix Books.

Hurowitz, V. (1992) *I Have Built You an Exalted House: Temple Building in the Bible in Light of the Mesopotamian and Northwest Semitic Writings*, Sheffield, England: Academic Press.

Interlinear Chumash (2008) 5 vols., Artscroll Series, Brooklyn: Mesorah.

Keil, C.F. and Delitzsch, Franz (1975) *Commentary on the Old Testament*, vol. 1, Grand Rapids: Eerdmans.

Kline, Meredith (1962) *Divine Kingship and Genesis 6:1-4*, Philadelphia Westminster Theological Journal, Vol., WTJ 24:2 May (187-204).

_____ (1965) *Oath and Ordeal Signs I*, Westminster Theological Journal 27.2 (115-39).

_____ (1999) *Images of the Spirit*, Eugene, OR: WIPF & Stock.

_____ (2000) *Kingdom Prologue: Genesis Foundations for a Covenantal Worldview*, Overland Park, KS: Two Age Press.

_____ (2006) *God, Heaven and Har Magedon: A covenantal Tale of Cosmos and Telos* Eugene, OR: WIPF & Stock.

_____ (2016) *Genesis: A New Commentary*, Peabody, MA: Hendrickson Publishers.

Lambert, WG (1975) *The cosmology of Sumer and Babylon, Ancient Cosmologies*, eds., C. Blacker and M. Loewe, London: Allen & Unwin Ltd.

Lang, B. (2002) *The Hebrew God: Portrait of an Ancient Deity*, New Haven, CT: Yale.

Lang, Martin (2008) *Floating from Babylon to Rome: Ancient Near Eastern Flood Stories in the Mediterranean world*. Innsbruck, Austria: Kaskal. Vol. 5.

Levenson, J. D. (1984) *The Temple and the World*, The Journal of Religion 64.3

_____ (1985) *Sinai and Zion: An Entry into the Jewish Bible*, New York: Harper & Row.

_____ (1988) *Creation and the Persistence of Evil: The Jewish Drama of Divine Omnipotence*. Princeton: Princeton University Press.

Longman, Tremper III & Walton, J. H. (2018) *The Lost World of the Flood*, Downers Grove, IL: IVP Academic.

Lopez, Raul (1998) *The Antediluvian Patriarchs and Sumerian King list*, Journal of Creation 12, no. 3 Dec. (347-357).

Lundquist, John M. (1984) *The Common Temple Ideology of the Ancient Near East, The Temple in Antiquity*, ed., T.G. Madsen, Provo, UT: BYU.

_____ (1994) *What is a Temple? A Preliminary Typology*, ed., Donald W. Parry, *Temples of the Ancient World: Ritual Symbolism*, Salt Lake City: Deseret books.

_____ (2002) *Fundamentals of Temple Ideology from Eastern Traditions, Reason, Revelation, and Faith: Essays in Honor of Truman G. Madsen*, ed., Donald W. Parry, Daniel C. Peterson, and Stephen D. Ricks, Provo, UT: FARMS.

_____ (2008) *The Temple of Jerusalem: Past, Present, and Future*, Westport, CT: Praeger.

Mafico, T.J. (1986) *The Ancient and Biblical View of the Universe*, Journal of Theology for Southern Africa no. 54:3.

Mallowan, M.E.L. (1964) *Noah's Flood Reconsidered*, Iraq Vol. 26 No. 2 Autumn (62-82) British Institute for the Study of Iraq.

Matthews, Victor H. (2002) *A Brief History of Ancient Israel*, Louisville, KY: WJK Press.

Malina, Bruce J. (2001) *The New Testament World: Insights from Cultural Anthropology*, Louisville, KT: WJK Press.

McCann, J.M. (2013) *Woven of Reeds: Genesis 6:14b as Evidence for the Preservation of the Reed-Hut Urheiligtum in the Biblical Flood Narrative*. In *Opening Heaven's Floodgates* ed., Jason M. Silverman, Piscataway, NM: Gorgias Press.

McGovern, Patrick E. (1997) *The Beginnings of Winemaking and Viniculture in the Ancient Near East and Egypt*, Expedition Magazine 39.1 online.

Mishnah (1989) trans., H. Danby, Oxford: Oxford University Press.

Morales, L. Michael (2012) *The Tabernacle Prefigure*, Walpole, MA: Peeters.

_____ (2015) *Who Shall Ascend the Mountain of the Lord?* Downers Grove, IL: Inter-Varsity Press.

_____ (2017) *House of God*, Tabletalk Magazine.com December.

Noegel, Scott B. & Rendsburg, Gary A. (2009) *Solomon's Vineyard: Literary and Linguistic Studies in the Song of Songs*, Atlanta: SBL.

Oppenheim, Leo (1944) *The Mesopotamian Temple*, Biblical Archaeologist, Vol. 7, No. 3 Sept.

_____ (1949) *The Golden Garments of the Gods*, Journal of Near East Studies, 8 (172-193).

Parpola, Simo (2012) *The Neo-Assyrian Royal Harem*, Wiesbaden, Germany: Harrassowitz Verlag (613-626).

Parrot, Andre (1953) *The Flood and Noah's Ark*, NYC: Philosophical Library.

Parry, Donald W. (1994) *Garden of Eden: Prototype Sanctuary*, ed., Donald W. Parry, *Temples of the Ancient World: Ritual Symbolism*, Salt Lake City: Deseret books.

Patai, R. (1967) *Man and Temple in Jewish Myth and Ritual*, NYC: KTAV Publishing.

_____ (1979) *The Messiah Texts*, Detroit: Wayne State University Press.

Pleins, J.D. (2003) *When the Great Abyss Opened: Classic and Contemporary Readings of Noah's Flood*, Oxford: Oxford University Press.

Podany, Amanda H. (2014) *The Ancient Near East: A Very Short Introduction* NYC: Oxford University Press.

Rendsburg, Gary (2006) *Moses as Equal to Pharaoh*, Jewishstudies. rutgers.edu

Sarna, N.M. (1970) *Understanding Genesis: The Heritage of Biblical Israel*, New York: Schocken.

_____ (1989, 2001) *Genesis: JPS Torah commentary*, Philadelphia: JPS.

Sailhammer, John H. (1992) *The Pentateuch as Narrative: A Biblical-Theological Commentary*, Grand Rapids: Zondervan.

Silverman, Jason M. (2013) *Noah's Flood as Myth and Reception: An Introduction*, Piscataway, NJ: Gorgias Press.

Skarsaune, Oskar (2002) *In the Shadow of the Temple*, Downers Grove, IL: IVP Academic.

Streett, Daniel (2007) *As it was in the Days of Noah: The Prophets' Typological Interpretation of Noah's Flood*, CTR 5, no. 1 (33-51).

Temple in Antiquity (1984) ed., T. G. Madsen, Salt Lake City, UT: Bookcraft.

The Complete Artscroll Siddur (1985), Brooklyn: Mesorah.

The Cosmic Mountain: Eden and Its Early Interpreters in Syriac Christianity (1988). *Genesis 1-3 in the History of Exegesis: Intrigue in the Garden,* ed., Gregory Allen Robbins (187-224). Lewiston, NY: Edwin Mellen Press.

The Old Testament Pseudipigrapha (1983-85), ed., J. H. Charlesworth, 2 vols., Garden City, NY: Doubleday.

The Psalms (1997) trans., R. Samson Raphael Hirsch, NYC: Feldheim.

The Works of Josephus (2000), trans., W. Whiston, Peabody, MA: Hendrickson.

The Works of Philo (1993), trans., C.D. Yonge, Peabody, MA: Hendrickson.

Thiele, Edwin R. (1983) *The Mysterious Numbers of the Hebrew Kings,* Grand Rapids: Kregel.

Tosefta (2002), 2 vols., trans., J. Neusner, Peabody, MA: Hendrickson.

Triolo, Joseph (2019) *The Tabernacle as Structurally Akin to Noah's Ark: Considering Cult,*

Cosmic Mountain, and Diluvial Arks in Light of the Gilgamesh Epic and the Hebrew Bible, Fullerton, CA: Society of Biblical Literature, March.

Van Leeuwen, Raymond C. (2007) *Cosmos, Temple, House: Building and Wisdom in Ancient Mesopotamia and Israel.* Ed., Richard Clifford, *Wisdom Literature in Mesopotamia and Israel,* No 36, Atlanta: Society of Biblical Literature.

Van Oudtshoorn, Andre (2015) *Mything the Point: The use of Mythology in Genesis 1-11,* Perth, Australia: Crucible 7:1 November.

Van Seters, John (1992) *Prologue to History,* Westminster John Knox Press: Louisville, KY.

Vavilov, N. (1937) *Asia: Source of Species,* Asia Feb. 113.

Vermes, Geza (1981) *Jesus the Jew,* Philadelphia: Fortress.

_____ (1997) *The Complete Dead Sea Scrolls in English,* London: Penguin.

Von Rad, Gerhard (1972) *Genesis: A commentary,* Revised. OTL. Philadelphia: Westminster Press.

Walsh, Brian J. (2014) *Subversive Christianity: Imaging God in a Dangerous Time,* Eugene OR: WIPF & Stock.

Walsh, Carey Ellen (2000) *The Fruit of the Vine: Viticulture in Ancient Israel*, Winona Lake, IN: Eisenbrauns.

Waltke, Bruce K (2001) *Genesis: A Commentary*. Grand Rapids: Zondervan.

Walton, J. H. (1995) *The Mesopotamian Background of the Tower of Babel Account and its Implications*, Bulletin for Biblical Research 5, 155-175.

_____ (2006) *Ancient Near Eastern Thought and the Old Testament*, Grand Rapids: Baker Academic.

Weinfeld, Moshe (1995) *Social Justice in Ancient Israel*, Jerusalem: Magnes Press.

Wenham, Gordon J. (1978) *The Coherence of the Flood Narrative*, Vetus Testamentum 28: (336-48).

_____ (1987) *Genesis 1-15*. WBC: 1. Nashville: Nelson.

Westermann, Claus (1974) *Genesis 1-11: A Commentary*, Minneapolis: Augsburg.

Widengren, G. (1957) *King and Covenant*, Journal of Semitic Studies 2.1 (1-32).

Wiercinski Andrzej (1976) *Pyramids and Ziggurats as the Architectonic Representations of the Archetype of the cosmic Mountain, Part 1* Almogaren 7 (199-210).

Wright, G. Ernest (1944) *The Significance of the Temple in the Ancient Near East: Part III The Temple in Palestine-Syria*, Biblical Archaeologist 7.3 (65-78).

Wright, N.T. (2012) *How God Became King*, NY: Harper Collins.

_____ (2016) *The Day the Revolution Began: Considering the Meaning of Jesus's Crucifixion*, NY: Harper Collins.

Yahuda, Abraham Shalom (1933) *The Language of the Pentateuch in its relation to Egyptian*, London: Oxford University press.

GLOSSARY

Adah – ornament
Adam – blood of G-d
Adamah – red, earth, ground
Adonai – Lord, substitute for YHWH
Amaru – flood
Arah – to pluck
Aron – Ark, box, coffin
Axis Mundi – world center, pole connects heaven and earth

Ba'al – master, Canaanite god
Banah – to build
Bat – daughter
Batsheva – daughter of seven, Bathsheba
Bavel – Babylon, Chaldea
Bet – second letter of Hebrew alphabet
Beit – house
Beit haMikdash – House of the sanctuary
Beit Pagey – House of unripe figs
Betenos – House of Refuge
Ben – son
Ben Adam – son of man
Ben Elohim – son of G-d
Benai – children, plural of son
Benai Israel – children of Israel
Beresheet – in the beginning, Genesis
Brachah – blessing
Brit – covenant, to cut
Brit Chadasha – renewed covenant, new covenant,
    New Testament

Brit Milah – covenant of cutting, circumcision
Bul (m'bul) – flood

Chag HaMatzah – Feast of Unleavened Bread
Chalil – to pierce, open
Chamor – male donkey
Chaoskampf – divine struggle
Chavah – Eve, mother of the living
Cheruvim – Cherubim, angelic beings

Dam – blood
Debir – Holy of Holies
Devar – speak
Din – judge

Echad – one
Edut – decrees, testimony
Eish – man
Eshah – woman
Eishet Chayil – Woman of Valor, Proverbs 31
El Elyon – God Most High
El Shaddai – God the mountain, almighty
Elohim – name for God, plural of El
Ephah – a measure
Eretz – earth, land
Etz – tree
Etzim – trees, bones
Etz Chaim – Tree of Life
Even Shettiyah – foundation stone, stone of drinking

Gahon – belly, stomach, gushing
Gan – garden
Gan Eden – Garden in Eden
Gephen – vine
Gihon – belly, gush, womb, spring in Jerusalem

Gibborim – strong ones, mighty
Goyim – nations

HaKodesh – the Holy Place
Har – mountain
Har'el – Mountain of God
HaShem – The Name used as a substitute for G-d's name in conversation
Hekal – sanctuary

Kadosh – holy, set apart, separate
Kanah – a possession, zealous, birds nest
Kaphar – pitch, cover, atonment
Kapporet – cover
Kedoshim – saints, holy ones
Kedushah – sanctified, dedicated, consecrated, set apart (can also be a harlot)
Kerem – vineyard
Ketonet – long-sleeved robe
Kinnim – rooms, stalks, branches
Kippur – atone
Kodesh – holy
Kodesh haKodeshim – Holy of Holies
Kohanim – plural for priests
Kohen – priests
Kohen Gadol – High Priest
Kometz – handful
Korban – offering, draw near

Lamed – 12th letter of Hebrew Alphabet
Livyathan – Leviathan
Luchot HaEven – Tablets of Stone

Ma'at – order
Malkut – kingdom

Malkut Shemayim – Kingdom of Heaven, Kingdom of G-d
Marad – to revolt, bitter
Mashal – parable, proverb, dominion, rulership
Maschiach – messiah
Matzah – unleavened bread
Mayim – water
Mayim hayim – living water
Melech – king
Menorah – seven-branched lampstand
Mikdash – Holiness
Minchah -grain offering
Mishkan – Tabernacle
Mitzvot – commandments
Mizbeach – altar
Moshe – Moses

Nephillim – fallen ones, giants
Niddah – separate, remove from camp
Noach – Noah, brings rest or comfort

Ohel Eduth – Tent of Testimony
Ohel Moed – Tent of Meeting
Olah – elevation or raised up offering

Parokhet – curtain, veil
Parousia – Greek: coming presence
Peredah – female wild donkey
Pesach – Passover

Rachaf – to hover, move, flutter as a bird
Rahav – broad, storm, proud
Reisheet – first, head, beginning
Rosh – head
Rosh Chodesh – head of the month
Rosh HaShanah – New Year, head of the year

Ruach – spirit
Ruach Elohim – Spirit of God
Ruach HaKodesh – Holy Spirit

Shabbat – Sabbath, seventh, rest
Shalom – peace
Shem – name
Shema – hear, Hear O Israel: opening words of the prayer
    proclaiming the unity of God
Shemayim – heavens
Shemot – Exodus
Sh'eol – grave, underworld
Sheva – seven, oath
Shiva – sitting, resting mourning for seven days
Shofar – ram's horn trumpet
Siddur – Hebrew prayer book
Soviv – a surround, middle
Sukkah – booth, temporary shelter
Sukkot – Feast of Tabernacles

Talmadim – disciples, students
Tamid – daily
Tamim – perfect, blameless, complete
Tanakh – Old Testament, Hebrew Scriptures
Tehillim – Psalms
Tehom – the waters of the deep, the abyss, chaos
Teshuvah – repentance
Tevah – ark, basket, chest, shrine
Tishri – seventh month on Hebrew calendar, usually in
    Sept./Oct.
Tohu – empty
Tov – good
Torah – instruction, law, first five books of the Bible
Tzaddik – righteous one
Tziyon – Zion

Tzemach – sprout
Tzva'ot – hosts

Vav – sixth letter of Hebrew alphabet
Vohu – without form

Yahweh – Hebrew name of G-d
Yam – sea
Yam Suph – Sea of Reeds
Yamim – days
YHWH – unpronounceable name of God, tetragrammaton
Yom – day
Yom haKippurim – Day of Atonements
Yom Echad – One day or Day One
Yom Teruah – Day of the Blast of the Shofar
Yeshua – Jesus
Yocheved – Glory of Yah
Yovel – Jubilee, release

Zigguratu – to be high or lifted up, ziggurat

THE TEMPLE REVEALED SERIES

The Temple Revealed in Noah's Ark (Vol. 3)

The story of Noah's Ark is one of the Bible's best-known. Is it just a quaint bedtime story? A major scientific marvel? An allegory? Was there a flood that covered the entire earth? Did a man named Noah build an extremely large boat and fill it with animals? Was the ark designed as a floating sanctuary? This book explores ancient Near East ideas through the lens of chaos and order. It looks at the cosmos as a kingdom, the mountain as the center of government, the ark as the bulwark against chaos, and the vineyard as a sign of new creation. This book takes the reader on a journey to discover the answers to some of the Bible's most perplexing questions about the days of Noah!

The Temple Revealed in the Garden (Vol. 2)

The Garden in Eden was filled with fruit-producing trees, sprouting plants and grasses, and gently flowing rivers. Adam, God's chosen king/priest, was called to cultivate the garden's fertile soil, to guard the sacred space from external enemies, and to rule over the earth. This book examines the Garden story from an ancient Near East perspective. It explores new ideas and concepts about the oldest story in the world and challenges the reader to think outside the box.

The Temple Revealed in Creation: A Portrait of the Family (Vol. 1)

The Bible is filled with Temple imagery and symbols that were likely understood by first century Christians. In this ground-breaking work, Dr. Dinah Dye explores the ancient understanding of the Temple from the birth of time. This book takes the reader back to the beginning in search of the true meaning of the Temple and its enduring relevance for today's family.

ABOUT THE AUTHOR

Dr. Dinah Dye was raised in Ottawa, Canada in a conservative Jewish home. Early on, she attended Hebrew school, celebrated the Sabbath and festivals in the Jewish community of Ottawa, and enjoyed summers at an orthodox Jewish camp. She spent her teen years and early twenties heavily involved in the New Age movement. Dinah concluded that the truth would be based on three things: it would be easy to understand, it would be for everyone, and it would be based on love. Dinah was a part of the 60/70s counterculture movement until she came to faith in Yeshua (Jesus) the Messiah.

Dinah has served in a variety of leadership positions with the Assemblies of God and Foursquare International, including as director of Foursquare's Bible Institute. She received her BS in Education and Business from Southwestern Assemblies of God University in Waxahachie, TX. Dinah's video teachings have aired on Israel TV Network in TX, BRAD TV in South Korea, Son Broadcasting in NM, and God's Learning Channel in Midland, TX.

Understanding the importance of connecting the Gospels and Epistles to the Hebrew Scriptures led to the creation of Dinah's ministry, Foundations in Torah. Dr. Dye holds a DMIN in Hebraic Studies in Christianity and has been examining Hebraic/Christian connections for over 40 years. She has led trips to Israel as well as numerous Passover celebrations for churches and local community groups. Audio/video teachings are available on her website.

Currently, Dinah is a regular programmer on Israel TV Network. Her video series Bonhoeffer: From Tyranny to Freedom, one of the network's main features, compares the rise of tyranny in 1930s Germany to the current climate in the USA. It has been one their most viewed videos. Her programs are also featured on the Hebraic Roots Network and Messiah Media.

Dinah's previous two books, The Temple Revealed in Creation: A Portrait of the Family and The Temple Revealed in Garden: Priests and Kings have consistently been best sellers on Amazon in the Messianic Judaism category. Both books have been translated into Spanish, and teachers from Puerto Rico, Columbia, Ecuador, and Peru have been sharing the material with their congregations.

Dinah hosts a podcast called Returning to Eden and serves as executive director of On Fire Prayer, an international prayer initiative calling the faith community to prayer and action. She speaks regularly at conferences and for local congregations throughout the United States and internationally. Dinah has also worked on several political campaigns in New Mexico and has been invited to speak at patriot rallies.

Dr. Dye's passion is to help students understand the Hebraic nature of the Scriptures within the ancient Near East cultural and historical tradition. Much of Dinah's research revolves around the Temple which she suggests is the framework for the Bible and an important key to bringing unity to a fractured community.

Dr. Dye and her husband Michael live outside Albuquerque, NM where they spend their free time with their grandchildren.

Foundations in Torah
www.FoundationsInTorah.com

On Fire Prayer
www.onFirePrayer.com

DinahDye@protonmail.com

Made in the USA
Coppell, TX
17 January 2024

27842060R00098